ISSAC J. BAILEY

Proud. Black. Southern.

(But I Still Don't Eat Watermelon in Front of White People.)

PUBLISHED BY STAR BOOKS
The Kansas City Star Co.
Kansas City, Mo.

Kansas City Star Books / Rockhill Books
The Kansas City Star
1729 Grand Blvd.
Kansas City, MO 64108

"Proud. Black. Southern. (But I Still Don't Eat Watermelon in Front of White People)"
Published by Star Books, Kansas City, Mo.

Cover art Artist/Designer/Typesetter: Keita S. Sullivan

Editing help: Mona Prufer and Sarah Kennedy
Special thanks: Trish O'Connor, Carolyn Murray, Jeffry Couch, The Sun News staff

First Edition

For more of Bailey's work, visit TheSunNews.com.

Manufactured in the United States of America

Library of Congress Control Number: 2008909582

ISBN-9781933466897

To Lyric, my heart
To Kyle, my soul
To Tracy, my world
To Fabrice, whom we'll never forget

Table of Contents
Preface

Obama

Blacks and Whites, Brothers and Sisters

Family

Preface

I don't recoil at the sight of a Confederate flag.

I don't want the statues celebrating Confederate soldiers and leaders removed from the State House or the State House grounds.

I understand the allure of Robert E. Lee, and watched the "Dukes of Hazzard" just as faithfully as my black and white Southern brothers and sisters.

I have a white friend who spent much of his life calling black people niggers – not in the good way – and felt it OK to treat some black employees as second-class citizens.

I'm a black man who was born in a rural part of South Carolina – where slaves were once plentiful – just four years after blacks finally secured universal suffrage in a country that says it was built on and in freedom.

I'm as proud of the South as I'm frustrated by it.

I love our heritage but am haunted by our history. I deplore the lack of measurable progress in our educational and criminal justice systems but am the first to beat back any outside attacks from those who measure us by our worst characteristics while ignoring the best, that we, too, produce world-class doctors and lawyers, chemists and literary giants, business titans.

I might not recoil at the sight of the flag but still catch myself involuntarily wincing, even as I've found ways to highlight the stories of those who love the flag but don't hate me or my dark skin.

I don't want the statues of known racists removed from public places – because many of the men they represent helped shape the South in important ways. But I want us to remember – and those statues to reflect – them in all their complexity, not watered-down versions suitable only for those who are in denial about the role slavery played in the Civil War.

And no, I haven't forgotten about that war, nor am I ashamed that it remains a Southern obsession. The blood of the more than 600,000 Americans who died in that war ran in our streets, stained the ground upon which we still walk.

We daily drive past plantations that held enslaved Africans. We get to know, from our earliest moments on Earth, of the atrophied cotton, rice and sugar cane fields upon which they worked because we can see those fields through our back windows. How can we forget when everywhere we go – and work and live and play – reminds of that horrible period?

And while I have a white friend who used to frequently use the word nigger, I respect him more because he changed after having a mirror held up to his behavior.

And I know that the entire country – from as close as the smell of collard greens emanating from Granny's restaurant to as far away as the sushi bars in Hollywood, California – is just as conflicted about race as the South. The only difference is that we admit it while many other Americans refuse to.

Others wonder why we continued to send former segregationist Strom Thurmond back to the U.S. Senate for half a century – the man who publicly vowed to keep Jim Crow alive while privately having an affair with a black woman – yet don't notice the face on the dollar bill. It's the face of the greatest American hero, George Washington, the man who was brilliant and brave and handsome and humble … and a slave owner.

Others don't seem to notice that there is no more American story than the Southern story, that there are no deeper roots, that without us there would be no them.

They don't seem to understand that we can be just as crooked or honest, dim-witted or intellectual, cold or kind as the rest of our countrymen, that the blood runs just as red, and just as warm, through our veins as it does theirs.

Such slights have convinced too many of us to exaggerate our progress, to ignore our remaining difficulties and to ignore the sins of our past. I've spent years trying to counter that tendency, to tell the truth in all its beautiful and horrible glory, even as I've struggled to live it out in my own life. I've spent too much time afraid of stereotypes, which is why I spent so many years afraid of eating watermelon in front of white people, and not enough time being myself.

My life is the quintessential Southern story, which makes it the quintessential American story.

I don't wear flag lapels or hoist the American flag from a pole in my front yard.

I haven't always been proud of my country and, given all of its complexities and faults, don't know how anyone ever could.

But I'm grateful that God chose to put me in this place at this particular time, to watch our country change, to study how it has evolved, to help it grow even more.

I'm grateful that I get to witness the making of the first black president, knowing that Southern voters – particularly in South Carolina, where I grew up, and North Carolina, where I received my higher education – were primarily responsible for solidifying the history-making campaign.

And I'm grateful this country has allowed me – forced me– to evolve right along with it.

That's what I've spent the past dozen years trying to illustrate in print, through personal stories and investigative reporting, and what I'm hoping shines through in the pages of this book.

Proud. Black. Southern.

The Gray World
of Race

Racism Hasn't Been My Biggest Obstacle

I WAS BORN AND RAISED in South Carolina, a boy with dark skin years after Jim Crow ruled the South.

I grew up in a house with eight brothers, two sisters and a couple of adopted siblings.

We all received free lunch.

I attended a poor rural high school — population 98 percent black — where some prospective white teachers were scared off by rumors of violent, disrespectful students.

I've long since stopped counting the days I've been laughed at, ridiculed, overlooked, underestimated, considered unintelligent.

I still vividly remember leaving job interviews knowing for certain I'd be turned down, despite my qualifications and work ethic.

At about this point in my retelling of this story for audiences and race relations courses I teach, several knowing smiles and nodding heads can be detected in the crowd, as if to say, "I know it must have been hell being a black man growing up in racist South Carolina."

But when I tell them that I've hardly ever faced racism, that most of my struggles and hurts were based on my more than 26 years of severe stuttering – not the color of my skin – the knowing smiles turn into confused stares.

I understand why.

Blackness so often has been defined by struggle, by pain, by anger, by the need to overcome impossible odds, it's hard to know where reality ends and hyperbole begins.

You'd think joy has never taken up residence in our hearts.

Racism has reached such mythical status that to even think of blacks, particularly Southerners, as having experienced anything other than hell seems almost blasphemous.

To allow yourself to imagine, even for one second, that things aren't as bad as some say, that there isn't a white man around every corner trying to knock you down, seems foreign.

— I've heard some say and I believed them for a long time — that a black man living in America who isn't angry doesn't know what time it is.

That racism is the scourge of the earth.

That no one can understand our plight.

They often remind me of this:

"The problem of the twentieth century is the problem of the color line," said W.E.B. Du Bois in 1903.

He spoke about a double consciousness, "A peculiar sensation. ...One ever feels this twoness an American, a Negro; two souls, two thoughts, two unreconciled strivings; two warring ideals in one dark body, whose dogged strength alone keeps it from being torn asunder."

But they don't recognize this:

That the problem of the 21st century may end up being the problem of the generation line.

My generation and those to come must be allowed – no forced – to free ourselves from the damning and limiting identity race has placed on our lives.

We haven't experienced the dogs and water hoses, haven't been blocked entrance to our favorite restaurants, and haven't witnessed our friends hanging from trees.

But we're expected to identify as though we had.

We are forced to toe the line between two worlds, one

refusing to let go, the other open to us like never before.

Our personal struggle trying to reconcile the two has become more powerful than the man in a hood or any racist employer.

But the voices in my head convinced me such thoughts were nonsense, made me a "sell-out."

They convinced me I would be redlined when searching for a house, be denied a mortgage and never be promoted.

And those voices are urging me to let you know racism isn't yet dead, that a colleague of mine on assignment was recently called a nigger, another treated like a criminal.

They are urging me to remind you of James Byrd.

For too long, those voices convinced me to feel guilty that I hadn't been pierced by the slings and arrows my parents and your parents fought successfully against.

I won't ignore those voices. But neither will I be beholden to them.

The Perils of Ignoring the Idiots

THE LETTER FROM the anonymous reader began subtly enough. Any hyper teenager armed with a first-grade vocabulary and a knack for silly troublemaking could have written it.

"Hey Issac JERK Bailey Who gives a rats ass about race and gender numbers!" it read.

Then it got a bit more serious.

"All you BLAK BASTARDS need to clean our white toilets. And you need to leave the newspaper. It should be ME with a column. But no your NAACP got you the job instead. I DARE you to have the balls to meet me outside your home (oh yes I know where you live!) at 8 PM next Monday night."

"Prepare for an ass kicking nigger."

It came in an unmarked envelope with no return address, as such letters often do. But it had a name, a "Ron Teague" from Conway, S.C. The police aren't sure such a man exists, and I'm not sure I did the right thing in alerting my supervisors about the letter, who then persuaded me to fill out a police report.

It's one of the most perplexing things about being a columnist — who happens to be black. What to do about the idiots? The idiots who represent a minority of the readership, but a vocal one? What to do with the stack of hate mail that grows by the year? Which silly threats do you dismiss out of hand? Which ones do you take seriously just in case? And how do you not let them affect what it is you know you must write?

What do you tell your wife, who has had to watch as her husband reveals personal information in the pages of a newspaper to discuss universal truths, even when they are painful, embarrassing even? Watch her husband be confrontational at times, conciliatory at others, knowing there are strangers who hate him for things he has written, for sure, but also solely because of the abundance of melanin in his skin?

What do you tell her when the Horry County Police Department decides it's best to send a patrolling police cruiser near your home — just in case — knowing a very real part of you wants the idiot to show up, to see if he really could make good on his threat?

What do you tell readers? Anything? Do you point out the irony, that about the time you received that letter, you were being accused of unnecessarily stirring up trouble, that you can't get past racism even though it no longer exists in any meaningful way because you dare to opine about the subject?

Do you tell them that you had to fuss and fight with your editors, who want desperately for you to be successful, to let you breathe, to decide for yourself, when it was best to deal with that topic versus myriad others as the paper's local columnist? Or that you followed a columnist who happened to be white and had to find a way to write for a readership that was also mostly white? Do you tell them that you appreciated their concern but was frustrated by it because you knew how to find your own way, to not allow yourself to become the "race columnist" or the "black columnist," given that you had spent more than three decades figuring out how best to cope in a world which seemed to desperately want to limit who you really are?

Do you tell those readers that you had long, heartfelt

discussions with your wife and a trusted colleague about leaving because you felt you weren't allowed to be fully yourself? Do you tell them you felt you weren't trusted enough to write about the local real estate market – something you had spent the past several years analyzing – or the growing number of layoffs in the manufacturing industry – something you had spent the past several years reporting – or the endless squabbling on Myrtle Beach City Council or the pampered live oak trees in Conway or the heroic everyday people – like the white woman who began caring for an elderly black man just because she thought it the right thing to do – or the pending hurricane season – when it was time to write about such things rather than race? Which is most of the time?

Do you tell them your back story, the one the letter writer obviously doesn't know, the one that proves that you earned your spot as the paper's main columnist, that you weren't chosen because they needed a black face and you were the first one they saw? Do you tell them about how you began as a part-time designer/part-time calendar clerk/part-time reporter earning a minimum salary?

Do you tell them that you forced your way into full-time reporting by pulling off a major project examining homelessness in the area, something the newspaper editors had long discussed but no one had stepped forward to do?

Do you tell them that you went from writing features about small towns, to covering city government and a bit of education? Do you tell them that you accepted a position as a business reporter, something for which you had no background and little understanding, but found a way to carve out the paper's first official, full-time real estate beat?

Do you tell them that you became business editor because you stepped forward, while still reporting, to fill in for the editor on his days off and days away, not because you wanted to, but because you knew it needed to be done?

Do you tell them that you won numerous awards and accolades along the way, tell them that you even helped others be better, too?

Or do you simply tell them that your name is Issac Bailey, that you were born in a small town — less than 1,000 residents — called St. Stephen, S.C. about 35 miles north of Charleston, S.C., where you attended an almost all-black, poor, rural high school before attending an almost all-white, rich, private college? That you are a husband and a father? That you've been a severe stutterer since the age of nine? That you have eight biological brothers, two sisters and a host of cousins who could almost pass as siblings?

That you write to inform, to entertain, to cause contemplation, to stir emotions, to spur action, to hold up a mirror, to reveal your story and the stories of others when they speak to a larger truth? That for you, writing about race is about all of those things, which is why it's a subject that needs illumination from multiple angles and levels and why it can't be summed up by the ugliness it causes or the beauty it elicits or the fear of being truthful it has spawned?

Do you tell them you have no ax to grind, that you aren't out to "stick it to the white man," as other anonymous readers have suggested? That you've vowed to purposefully offend no one while not shying away from potentially offending everyone?

After receiving that letter, I think I've told the world, through my column, all of those things. Not always directly, mind you, and sometimes too directly. I've done so because it's hard to be static in a world in which your skin tone makes you a "minority." I've gone through stretches where I purposefully decided to not write about race to prove that I was mainstream, without realizing such an attitude suggests that to be unashamedly black is to be a stranger, a foreigner, in your own land. It is not.

I've gone through stretches during which I believed

mentioning race, under any circumstance, was ultimately detrimental. It's not. I've gone through stretches during which I wanted to write things in precisely the way I wanted to, with no regard for my audience. They needed the truth. I needed to give it to them. It was up to them to be smart enough and tough enough to take it. That was dumb.

And I've gone through stretches during which I proudly kept a stack of racist hate mail, saw it as a badge of courage, of strength. That was useless, particularly given most in my audience either loved me or hated me for what I wrote and how I wrote it, even when they got angry with me, not for the color of my skin. I threw away that stack after realizing I was paying too much attention to the relatively few idiots and not enough to the majority that wanted to be engaged, to be challenged, on this and so many other issues.

That's when I grew. That's when I decided not to write a column about that letter, or the half dozen or so others that came on its heels that I never got to read because they were redirected straight to the police department.

But I still wonder whether I made the right decision. To talk about the idiots might give them the momentary belief that they are more powerful than they really are, to give them credence. To not talk about them is to help create a false picture, that they no longer exist, that they aren't out there, that the issue of race is still only being discussed by those who benefit from "stirring the pot."

To ignore them is to leave the impression that columnists like me who happen to be black highlight every slight and happily scream about a racial boogeyman behind every bush when in fact, we do just the opposite or couldn't fulfill our larger duties.

It almost feels like lying. But how do you balance the concerns? Do you write about the large, local hotel complex that is being sued by a white employee who said she witnessed racist behavior, but the only proof she can provide is a muddled tape recording of a conversation that can barely be heard? Do you write about it, knowing the stain such accusations cause, no matter how untrue they may be? Or do you ignore it, knowing you could be unwittingly turning a blind eye to racism if you're wrong?

Do you expose the governmental department that is supposedly headed by a man overheard speaking in racial stereotypes? Or do you ignore it, knowing your source has no proof to back up his claims and wouldn't allow you to use his name?

Do you tell readers about the caller who said she knows a few prominent businessmen play a game every year in which the prize is a black lawn jockey. But she won't give her name, or theirs.

Do you tell them about the other caller, who called the newsroom to claim that you are flashing a secret gang sign in your column photo? Or do you, as I did, laugh it off and move on?

In the end, you check out the charges, and every other one like them — and they are frequent — and decide against writing about most because the evidence isn't clear enough or strong enough to outweigh the potential harm that could arise from a publicized false accusation.

And every time you make that call, you wonder whether it was the right one, if you haven't somehow succumbed to the constant pounding, about how your skin tone makes you susceptible to believing race is a factor when it isn't. You wonder if you've subconsciously given in, if you've only made things worse.

And every time you get accused of being too race-focused, you want to scream, to tell them all the work you do behind the scenes, that deciding what doesn't get reported is one of the hardest parts of our jobs, especially concerning this issue. You want to tell them about all the cases and complaints and charges you've investigated, to prove that you think deeply and care deeply, to prove that when you bring a claim to their attention that it means something, that it shouldn't be dismissed out of hand.

But you don't. You smile. You continue writing. You continue investigating. And you continue making judgment calls, based on your professional training and your need to balance the scales of justice.

And you hope you've done right by your readers, by your race, that you've been able to properly deal with the idiots when appropriate, to highlight their still looming, ugly power, or to dismiss them out of hand, to make sure you don't give them voice.

Race Gets In The Way Of Common Sense

BLACKS ARE HYPOCRITES because they are up in arms when whites say the word nigger but barely notice when a rap star sings it.

The Confederacy was a good thing because it helped end slavery.

The NAACP should stop focusing on the Confederate flag and be more concerned about its own people.

Blacks are trying to take privileges away from whites, and black leaders need to clean up their own backyards before trying to change whites.

You can imagine my discomfort as I listened to a reader who called and, politely enough, uttered those words in response to my January 14th column, a column, dare I remind you, about people's fear to fight discrimination and two white female friends of mine who are wonderful yet imperfect beings.

But if I had not listened, bitten my tongue, humbled myself, I would have never heard this a few seconds before our conversation ended:

"Sometimes we lose focus that would stereotype or point to someone as your enemy, when the enemy is all around and the enemy is an attitude," 43-year-old David from Myrtle Beach told me. "That attitude exists in all of us if it is allowed to grow and not pointed out, not just in white people. The enemy is the attitude, not the person. I feel like white people are made out to be the enemy all the time, when

11

it's not the color. That's what racism was all about in the first place."

Well said. Couldn't have said it better myself.

It took us 30 minutes to get there, though. Took ignoring the slowly boiling blood running through my veins, the angry twitching of my nose, the not-so-Godlike thoughts getting comfortable as they settled in my brain.

It took us that long to get there because I kept interrupting him, trying to take him to task for the inaccuracies and generalizations.

It took me a long time to start listening.

If it had been a few years earlier, when I knew everything and felt everyone who disagreed knew nothing, I would have lashed into him like a cheetah into a gazelle.

I would have sat on that phone for hours if necessary – ask my wife if you doubt it – yelled, kicked, screamed, danced a thousand jigs, jogged 10 miles with the phone attached to my ear, ate lunch, dinner and a light midnight snack, sent a colleague out for pills to keep me awake to make sure David knew the world was ending because of his stupidity, while not too subtly huffing with righteous indignation.

I would have gotten my point across no matter what it would have taken.

If not, I would have sat quietly and ignored him while I listened before hanging up and branding him racist, uninformed. And both of us would have been the worse for it, for I never would have realized David and I agreed on far more than we disagreed, never would have heard him say he was grateful I wrote the column because it stirred something deep within.

Made him uncomfortable but ready to consider things anew.

I would not have remembered he was a child of God, no better or worse than I.

He never would have gotten the chance to tell me it pained him deeply that our state and its residents look like the worst kind of racists because of the debates and constant back and forth rhetoric.

It pains me, too.

It pains me that we are so busy defending ourselves and beliefs that we've forgotten how to help in the healing. We're trying so hard to prove ourselves right, we've forgotten that it's more important to make things right.

It's a hard thing to do, live by that creed. Hard to, as my pastor says, look at the other person as a soul God wants, a soul God loves.

I don't know whether I taught David anything or helped him see why his initial comments would offend the many who feel marginalized like unequal partners in the game of life.

I learned, though, that somewhere beneath the misunderstandings and offensive comments is a place we can gather to advance God's kingdom.

We have to be willing to dig until we reach it.

I'm willing.

Are you?

Living proof that welfare does work

FOOD STAMPS DIDN'T cripple my family. They helped make ends meet.

Twelve years of free lunches in school didn't make me disdain education. They provided nourishment.

"Kaboom!" cereal through the WIC program and boxes of government cheese and distasteful, powdered government milk didn't make us lazy.

They helped us survive.

It's more than a decade after the landmark Welfare reform legislation and a common refrain has developed: welfare rolls have been successfully reduced because former recipients were forced to work, proving welfare made people dependent on government, made them crave an endless stream of handouts.

In other words, made them lazy.

Maybe the reform has been wildly successful, as most observers are saying. Or maybe an increased burden has been unfairly shifted onto poor, single parents, as some critics say.

I'll let the analysts and Bill Cosby debate those finer points because I want to make another one.

There was never a day our parents sat us down and said "Don't do well in school" because we would lose our so-called victim status. They worked us so hard at home – building rooms onto our house, chopping wood, helping our father make car repairs, picking tobacco and cucumbers –

14

school felt like a vacation, a refuge, a place we wanted to be all the time.

There was never a moment our parents told my sisters or brothers to produce babies out of wedlock so we could get more government handouts. They said what most responsible parents say: Delay sexual activity as long as possible, or be smart about it if we were foolish enough to ignore that warning.

"Until these people learn some responsibility for their own actions, they will keep expecting more and more from anybody but themselves. You liberals need to change your playbook because your old one is not working, and, quite frankly, more and more people are getting tired of it," an unnamed reader said in an e-mail in response to a column about a Georgetown woman's plans to "give" people affordable housing. I'm sure he would make the same point about welfare. "There is no accountability, responsibility ... on behalf of the individuals who receive these handouts. This junk has been going on for over forty years with no significant results. Can't you left-wing liberals understand ... all these entitlement, welfare, handout-type programs will never work."

They worked for me.

Intelligence Not Based On Just One Score

I READ A WASHINGTON POST ARTICLE about the importance of the SAT, about how George Mason University professor Walter E. Williams and others believe high school students should not apply to colleges where average SAT scores are at least 200 points higher than theirs.

Such talk brought back memories of some of my most challenging days, during which I foolishly hoisted the weight of the entire black race upon my back.

In the fall of 1991, I sat in Psychology 101 holding the 48 I received on my first-ever college exam. I'd felt alone before while attending Davidson College, with its 92 percent white student population whose average SAT was about 1300.

Mine was 1000.

But the loneliness that day was frightening.

I stared at the 48 as fellow students folded their 80s and 90s — the class average was 88 — placed them into book bags and left class as they often did, smiles dripping from their faces, jokes and laughter rolling from their lips.

I hurriedly left as well, trying to blend into the sea of white students in which I was the only black.

It was a foreign experience all around.
In high school, all but a handful of my classmates were black.

In high school, I excelled — in sports, socially, academically.

I graduated fourth in my class from the small school in St. Stephen, where advanced placement classes were nonexistent and chemistry labs consisted of a teacher standing in front of us making homemade ice cream.

We prepared for the SAT on an outdated computer that ran an obsolete test prep program. I'd always feared the day of the 48 would come, when I'd be found out as a fraud, unable to compete with the white geniuses, when my intellect would be overmatched.

I dreaded becoming another statistic, another in a long line of black students who leave high school with an over-inflated resume before flunking out in shame. Another shining example of the ineptness of the black race, I thought people would deem me.

I'd lived in my black skin for more than 18 years by that point, but never did it fit so snugly, never did it make me question my worth as much.

Even if those images resided only in the deep recesses of my brain, they felt real.

So real they almost blinded me into believing there was some profound reason why I cried that night as others played. Why I failed when others excelled.

I had heard the comments in high school from parents of rival Macedonia High School, where the student body was predominantly white. When talk of merging the two schools surfaced, they spoke of the violent tendencies we would bring, the unprepared minds.

"An 'A' student at St. Stephen couldn't make 'Cs' at Macedonia," a mother reasoned, not hiding her disgust for students she never met, a school she never visited.

At the time, I was angry, not only because of what she said but because part of me hoped — not believed — she was wrong.

The National Honor Society awards, the 1990 S.C. Governor's School appointment, the scholarship offers, none of it was able to flush that thought from my head. And at first, the 48 confirmed it, proved I wasn't capable, proved people like me couldn't compete.

It took me awhile to realize the 48 had little to do with my background, or skin tone, nothing to do with the demons tugging at my soul, wanting me to accept inferiority, took me a while to remember the home in which I grew, where excellence was a prerequisite, and the teachers who demanded my best. The 48 would have brought me crashing down, rather than thrust me forward, had it not been for them.

Yet it never ceases to amaze me that so many are willing to deem you unintelligent or unprepared based on a single score.

But it's most amazing when you are all too willing to do it to yourself.

Lying to Myself Only Built Anger

FOR THE LONGEST TIME, I was angry with white women. At least the ones who hurriedly locked their car doors, the ones who clutched their purses a little tighter as I approached.

It was one of my biggest complaints about being a black man in America, that I was viewed as a criminal first, complex human being last, if at all. Never mind that I rarely met such women. I can probably count on one hand the number of times someone scurried away when they saw my big, dark-skinned frame coming their way.

Still, that me-against-the-world attitude was intoxicating because it allowed me, in a sense, to control others, or at least control how I thought others saw me. It became a de facto badge of honor.

But that attitude was sinister because I was so busy trying to protect myself from demons unseen that I ended up creating many of those that haunted me. The angrier I grew, the more I hoped to find people who would discriminate against me, sort of a perverse attempt to feel courageous.

When I applied for a mortgage, I expected the lender to deny my application or cheat me because of my dark skin. When I searched for a house, I expected the agent on duty to tell me all the homes had been sold. When I entered any gathering where I was one of the only – or the only – dark-skinned person, I was always on the lookout for the person who would be the first to call me nigger.

19

It was a distressing way to live, particularly because once I found what I was looking for – if only once or twice every few years – that slight became my focus, maybe for weeks, even months. And during those times, the air would feel a bit more stale, the sun dimmed. My entire perspective would be compromised, and happiness became hard to hang on to.

Even as I type this, I feel an invisible tug at my fingers, urging me to stop typing because of the fear that many will read this and use it as an indictment of other black males who have legitimate gripes.

Those who are forever being followed around in department stores by security guards. Those who are pulled over 20 times a year by rogue police officers for no other reason than being black. Those who are denied jobs and opportunities and serve longer sentences and continue to face a daily barrage of slings and arrows from the most vile racists, some of whom have skin as dark as their own.

Because I fear readers will do to me what I was doing to white women. I was throwing my expectations onto them and multiplying them by infinity to complete the lie that I wanted to believe — that everyone around me didn't see me, but rather their image of a criminal. I hated them for something I was doing to myself.

I was the liar because I spent most of my time trying not to become a victim of racism while all the while pretending to be one.

But I fear that many will read these words and use them as an excuse to no longer hear those still in pain, use me as an example, as proof, that racism is nothing more than the figment of millions of people's imaginations. Use me to soothe their conscience. Use me to deny their God-mandated obligation to demand equality for all.

Such fear once led me to think there was honor, even necessity, in telling others that I as a black man was an endangered species in America. To do otherwise would have felt like trampling on the experiences of others.

But I type, anyway, because my experiences and viewpoints are just as important, for they help shed light in dark places.

Walking in lock step to validate others doesn't help them or me; it only entraps us all.

Which is why I must apologize to all those white women. I judged them without knowing them, without stopping to ask myself if they were simply trying to protect themselves in a world that has grown too violent, or if the reason they clutched their purse tighter today was because they were mugged yesterday.

I must apologize because while I was despising them for denying my existence and all my complexities, I was denying theirs.

Race, History and Justice

My Answer To Reader's Comments

WHILE REMEMBERING ROSA PARKS...
I need to say something that many of you would
rather not be reminded of: Horry County is overwhelmingly
white. Pick a restaurant, a classroom, a social event, a gym,
a business, and make a mental note of the race of the doctors,
teachers, lawyers, real estate agents, waitresses, council
members, chamber of commerce leaders, bankers and bank
tellers, co-workers, church members, readers and employees
of The Sun News.

Check out the pictures of the people who stare back at
you from the walls. The vast majority of them are white.

That's not a complaint, just a fact. Not a cry for help,
just an observation. It isn't about racism or discrimination. It
doesn't mean I feel oppressed or put upon.

It means that people who look like me spend most of
their time in the minority, except when they go to church or
are at home.

Again, pointing that out isn't a sinister attempt to
make you feel uncomfortable or to elicit feelings of guilt.

It simply is what it is.

The reason I mention it today is because of the
reaction a few readers had of my recent column on Atlantic
Beach. The column included this line: "A revitalized
Atlantic Beach could be marketed as the only remaining all-
black tourist resort on the Eastern seaboard."

Some asked if I'm in favor of segregation if it's black

people who are doing the segregating. A reader from New Jersey asked, "Is Atlantic Beach going to remain a place for 'you' folks and Myrtle Beach for 'us' folks?"

Here's my answer:

I am not in favor of anyone segregating themselves, and I believe knocking down those barriers on Ocean Boulevard would be a good thing. And everyone, regardless of race, should be allowed to work or live in or visit the town.

But I understand why the town wants to hold onto its heritage. I understand because every other place its residents work and play puts them in the minority. It is understandable to want to be part of the majority. Being part of the majority makes some so comfortable they hardly ever have to notice that they are.

If you have a problem with Atlantic Beach being all or mostly black, do you also have a problem with Horry County being mostly white?

There was a disgusting form of racial segregation designed to demean a whole group of people, the kind Rosa Parks became famous for fighting.

Don't assume all racially homogenous settings are evidence of an attempt to hold onto that ugly past.

Few Recall Orangeburg Massacre

STANDING WITH HUNDREDS of black and white people for the grand opening of the replica of the Myrtle Beach Colored School, my mind wandered to 1968, to S.C. State University, where three students were shot dead by state troopers and up to 30 injured.

It was the first shooting of unarmed students on a college campus by government officials in U.S. history.

Students had built a bonfire to protest a bowling alley's policy to exclude blacks. A few threw rocks and such. An officer was hit by one of the projectiles and fell backward. Several minutes lapsed before they began firing wildly into the crowd.

That is a condensed and overly simplified account. I hope you take the time to learn more. But you might have a hard time. The Horry County Public Library System, I was told, has only one copy of ``Orangeburg Massacre,'' which recounts what happened. Barnes & Noble on Seaboard Street in Myrtle Beach has to special order them. I was schooled in South Carolina, but we were not taught about the incident.

There seems to be little interest in the story. The state has never issued an official apology or conducted an official investigation. Only one person – a civil rights activist who was pardoned 25 years later – ever spent a day in jail.

I should give credit to Gov. Mark Sanford, the first governor to apologize and to say the incident was a blight on the state's history. But after speaking with him about it a few weeks ago, I can't. He believes opening an investigation might make the state legally culpable.

"You can't change history. No matter how bad it was, no matter how good it was, it's gone," he said. "You apologize, you ask for forgiveness, you try to learn from that, you say I'm not ever going to do that again, and you take steps to make sure you never do."

Sort of like what North Carolina spent the past six years doing. Officials there commissioned an investigation of an 1898 massacre of blacks by an angry white mob in Wilmington and made recommendations to make amends – to make sure the story was never forgotten.

That's why I was proud to attend the grand opening of the Colored School. Because it showed that people here aren't afraid of doing something to make sure an important part of our painful history is never forgotten.

The governor said we must "try to learn from" the tragedy. What can the state learn while its leaders ignore that it even happened?

The governor's apology seemed bold a few years ago. It rings more hollow with every passing year.

White Guilt Obstructs Justice

I DON'T CARE ABOUT WHITE GUILT.

I used to. But I found such sympathy to be as unhealthy as white guilt itself, which is the kind of guilt that drives white people to unwittingly paint blacks with an overly sympathetic brush, to deny their own pain and retreat behind an impenetrable wall that makes honest cross-cultural exchanges impossible. It keeps them on a fruitless search for conflict-free relationships.

It's the kind that drives too many white people to wear uncomfortable, pained smiles while in the company of blacks, all the while fearing if they say the wrong word or allow the wrong thought to work its way through their brains, they'll be labeled racist or worse – that they would add to the so-called unfair burden blacks face for being black.

But mainly I no longer care about such guilt because I've learned it is one of the biggest impediments to social justice. Because it often turns into anger and denial, the kind of which I'm sure prompted a few readers to write me after a recent column in which I detailed why I was saddened by South Carolina's refusal to commission an official investigation into the "Orangeburg Massacre."

Thirty-eight years ago, S.C. state troopers killed three unarmed S.C. State University students during the height of a tense protest over an Orangeburg bowling alley's segregation policy.

Some believe the officers' actions must have been

27

justified. One reader said I was trying to make him feel guilty, said I need to just get over it, as if justice has an expiration date.

I don't care if you feel guilty. I only care that you are made aware. How you respond is up to you. But this is important. If our elected leaders showed the courage to right that wrong, it could go a long way in beating back decades of suspicion too many blacks feel toward police officers.

Dealing forthrightly with the 1968 Orangeburg Massacre could help increase support for some of today's most contentious issues, such as school choice because a lot of the opposition is rooted in the fear that school choice is an attempt to resegregate schools in the way some white families reacted to the desegregation of the '60s and '70s. They left public schools and created a system of private ones.

The massacre may have happened 40 years ago, but it and the racial unrest that caused it linger over the state like a cloud ready to unleash a storm on a state unwilling to deal with its ugly past.

Memories of History Often Selective

IT WAS SUPPOSED to be about honor, and maybe it was. Thousands in my native South Carolina spent a week celebrating the eight dead Confederate soldiers who were aboard history's first submarine to sink an enemy ship.

It culminated with a funeral procession led by our top state senator dressed as a Confederate officer. A newspaper account said, "The crewmen of the Hunley were immortalized as American heroes." Maybe they were.

And all the festivities supposedly made many South Carolinians proud. Maybe they did.

I've tried for years now to ignore it. The denial. I live in a place where those who fought to save slavery are hailed for bravery while their flawed loyalty is excused.

I live in a place where flying Confederate flags over public property is seen as a birthright.

Those who deny the horrors of the Holocaust are rightly laughed out of town. But where I live, those who trumpet the lie that the Civil War wasn't about slavery are elected to the state's highest offices.

They even ignore the words of their heroes.

After losing the war, Confederate President Jefferson Davis and Vice President Alexander Stephens said it wasn't about slavery. But at the beginning of the conflict, Davis said they took up arms to beat back the North's insistence on choking off the institution. Stephens, in a March 21, 1861, speech, said this, excerpted in Kenneth Stampp's "The

Causes of the Civil War":

"Our new government ... its foundations are laid, its cornerstone rests, upon the great truth that the Negro is not equal to the white man; that slavery, subordination to the superior race, is his natural and moral condition. This, our new government, is the first, in the history of the world, based upon this great physical, philosophical, and moral truth..."

The place I live is, yes, the South in the 21st century.

But I also live in these United States, a place where many scoff at outdated Southern traditions but are happy to honor former slave owners, put their faces on currency, build statues in their likeness.

All of America does for Thomas Jefferson and George Washington what Confederate sympathizers do for Davis and Stephens. So yes, many of my fellow South Carolinians spent a week honoring those who fought for an evil cause.

But such selective historical remembrance isn't simply a Southern obsession. It's an American tradition.

A Southern, Civil War Reality Check

I'M A BAD SOUTHERNER.

That's the consensus of readers who didn't like that I reminded them the South fought for slavery.

First, some of my detractors' most legitimate points (though most missed the larger point, which was that we all have selective memories about our heroes):

The North didn't take up arms to end slavery. That was added two years into the conflict. In fact, Abraham Lincoln said blacks were inferior and that white supremacy was natural.

Most Southerners didn't own slaves, and some slave states remained a part of the union – which helped them retain slaves for a short time after Lincoln's Emancipation Proclamation. In fact, Lincoln ordered his generals to return runaway slaves.

Slavery was common in many parts of the world. Africans helped sell other Africans and there were black slave owners. One of the richest lived in South Carolina, in Sumter County.

Slavery was legal.

"May the souls of all that died in the Civil War for the South haunt and torment you for the rest of your life without pause," one well wisher said.

OK, that final point wasn't legitimate. But it was funny.

Now a reality check:

Fact: The president and vice president of the Confederacy, as well as those who penned the papers of secession, said clearly that preserving slavery was the reason for the war. Several editorials in leading Southern newspapers said the same. And all of the other so-called reasons for the war – state's rights, economics, etc. – hinged on slavery.

Fact: Most Southern soldiers didn't own slaves. But front-line soldiers never determine when or why to go to war. Leaders do.

Fact: Because slavery was once an acceptable practice does not lessen its evilness. Plenty of people, including many Southerners, spoke out against it and fought for its end at the height of the institution.

Fact: Poor Southern soldiers were in essence fighting to remain second-class citizens. Non–property owning whites for the first time got the vote after it was extended to blacks because the South lost the war.

Fact: It is silly to distill down the rich history of the South to a four-year period that ended in 620,000 deaths and kept this region in economic doldrums from which we are only now recovering.

Fact: Being a proud Southerner should mean more than romanticizing and mythologizing a war.

Duke Case Testifies To Inequalities

I QUESTIONED WHETHER an impartial jury would have enough evidence to render a guilty verdict in the Duke University lacrosse rape scandal case.

If the prosecutor didn't have any bombshells, I thought after reading multiple-detailed accounts about the case, this sad story must be put behind us.

But don't let the hype blind you to the importance of that case: It was a lot like the O.J. Simpson trial in what it revealed about our criminal justice system.

While money and privilege shouldn't give people license to unfairly prosecute you, they often are the only things that buffer defendants against unfair prosecution.

The defendants in this case were from the privileged class. They received top-notch legal counsel and invaluable public relations guidance.

A Socastee, S.C. man charged with homicide by child abuse, Wesley Smith, sat in a jail cell more than four years after he was charged and before it reached a courtroom. He also underwent hours of interrogations without a lawyer.

I know certain cases are slowed for a variety of reasons. I also know Smith wasn't as fortunate as former Enron executive Jeffrey Skilling, who was allowed to remain free pending appeals even after being sentenced to 24 years in prison.

The Kynande Bennett case, which involved a 4-year-old Conway, S.C. girl whose mother was convicted of aiding and abetting a homicide by child abuse and sentenced to 20 years, dragged along for several months with no movement. Bennett was reported missing Sept. 29, 2002. That case didn't make it to court for more than two years.

During the trial, the police said they interrogated Bennett's mother for several hours late one night without a lawyer present. Two experienced detectives grilled her in one room while a prosecutor stood feet away in another.

What they got that night – she supposedly nodded in the affirmative when asked if she killed her daughter – was among the strongest evidence against her. But the jury wasn't allowed to decide for themselves if it really was a nod or a nervous tick, as her lawyer said, because it wasn't video recorded. South Carolina doesn't require such videotaping even though the Innocence Project said it is one sure-fire way to reduce the number of wrongly convicted people only now being uncovered.

Had Bennett been a part of the privileged, like the Duke defendants, O.J. or Skilling, that likely would not have happened.

The Duke players deserve our sympathy because they were falsely accused. They were innocent. But our focus should remain on ridding our justice system of blatantly obvious inequities.

Whiplash Over Comment Goes Too Far

ALL OF THIS OVER a shock jock who said something shocking? Or not so shocking, given that he's spent the past three decades saying things more incendiary than "nappy-headed hos."

These are the times I hate the media. We are supposed to put things into context and measure our commentary. But instead of taking advantage of the opportunity to begin a contextually rich dialogue, too many media members – including the governing body of the National Association of Black Journalists – are fanning flames that don't need fanning.

We should be using this moment to point out the widespread racial hypocrisy in our country. We should be telling people that such overreaction is reason why an in-depth race dialogue is almost impossible.

We should note how the pendulum has swung too far, that the days when blacks had to watch their Ps and Qs or risk being harshly punished by race-based fear-mongers have been replaced by a growing fear by too many whites for the same reason. Even the great Rush Limbaugh succumbed to that new reality in the aftermath of comments he made while employed by ESPN. He fled instead of taking the fire to help force the pendulum back.

We should be taking note of the contradictions, particularly when civil rights leaders and others say they want white people to be open and honest but hammer them the moment they are.

We should remind people that most, if not all, of us have used language that could be considered racist when others weren't around. If someone hid a tape recorder or video in my house – or your house – we'd be labeled racist for making off-color jokes worse than the one that ignited this controversy.

My fellow journalists of color are just as guilty as everyone else.

Shouldn't we be talking about the appropriateness of that, rather than demanding that someone be fired? Isn't a week of self-flagellation, public flogging and a two-week suspension more than enough punishment for this particular crime? That it's not is proof that race relations have gotten so good that we've lost our ever-living minds.

We went from fighting to provide true freedom to all U.S. residents to acting as though it's the Apocalypse anytime someone says anything that can be construed as insensitive or racist.

If the worst racism the women of the Rutgers basketball team will have to endure is a racist joke by an overrated talk show host, they should thank their lucky stars.

And so should the rest of us.

Exit Niche, Change The World

THE REV. AL SHARPTON CAN CHANGE the world today – if he joins forces with the former Duke lacrosse players who were wrongly accused of rape. Together they can help re-establish the lost ideal of innocence until proven guilty and fight justice system inequalities.

The boys were unfairly demonized, and Sharpton years ago led protests in a rape case that turned out to be a hoax. Symbolically they would make a powerful team that would be hard to ignore.

The Rev. Jesse Jackson can change the world today – if he publicly forgives Don Imus. Jackson years ago was caught saying ``Hymietown.'' Imus is roasting in the aftermath of his own racist comments. No better pair could illustrate the power and purpose of forgiveness.

The Rutgers' women's basketball team could change the world – if its members began a speaking tour on high school campuses and told young girls they are not the helpless victims a sympathetic public is trying to make them out to be.

No one is in a better position to help the younger generation recognize that being called a dirty name today is almost nothing in comparison to the days when black men were lynched in the public square. What better way to illustrate that young people can – and will – determine their own worth, no matter the circumstance, no matter what some strange man behind a microphone says.

Black people could change the world today – if more of us began to believe that there is no shame in nappy, kinky hair. Too many of us believe the lie that only particular skin tone and hair textures make you beautiful.

CBS Corp. can change the world today – if now that it has fired Imus, it also pressures its colleagues at the Black Entertainment Network to stem the tide of demeaning videos flooding the airwaves. If it's not acceptable for an old white man to make disparaging remarks, it shouldn't be acceptable for young black ones to make them either.

What's more demeaning? A shock jock making a joke about "nappy-headed hos"? Or a video by a top black rapper smiling into the camera while placing a credit card in an intimate part of a half-naked black woman's body?

Activists can change the world today – if they realize that getting loudmouths fired won't advance equality. It is like trying to defeat terrorism by trying to shoot all the terrorists. It may resemble progress but only makes the fight harder.

You can change the world today – if you love when others demand you hate. The world won't change until we elevate selfless courage above moral outrage.

Racial
Awakening

I Resented Jesus

"SUBMIT TO ONE another out of reverence for Christ."
Ephesians 5:21

I resented Jesus Christ.

Didn't feel comfortable having those blue eyes stare back into my brown eyes from a wall in the church. Didn't like the long, blond hair – the image that suggested I should bow down and worship a man everything and everyone was telling me was nothing like me.

He didn't have my dark skin or large lips. Didn't have my history. Slave owners used that face to justify slavery, then used it to keep the slaves from rebellion.

Jesus' image resembled those I had seen in the Christian Knights of the Ku Klux Klan of South Carolina. I couldn't relate. Didn't want to. So I resented him, but couldn't put my finger on exactly why until I watched the Discovery Channel's "Jesus: The Complete Story."

It is there I saw a dark face with a large protruding jaw and big lips topped with black, Afro-like hair.

He still didn't look like me, and the show's producers didn't claim it was His face, only the closest scholars, historians and scientists could come to reproducing it.

And it is after that show I came to realize something I long suspected: the physical image of Jesus shouldn't matter in my walk with Him.

But it did, for a long time, and I suspect it continues to matter in the minds of too many.

I've already heard the screams from some who saw clips of the show, about how their tradition was being shattered, how tampering with the image of Jesus was blasphemous.

"How dare they," I can just hear them say, "desecrate Jesus by putting a dark-skinned face on Him."

I'm tempted to detail all the reasons a dark skin Jesus makes sense. But as I told you earlier, it doesn't matter.

What matters is how we have become so beholden to certain images, certain themes and traditions that we no longer seem overly concerned about the call God has on our life.

And if you think it's just your neighbor's problem, or the problem of the strange men and women you pass on street, stop for a moment and take inventory of your community, your school, your job... your church.
We find it easy to think things are the way they are because they are the way they're supposed to be.

We've all heard it, probably said it, that blacks shout and worship God differently than whites. That the music is different. The dress is different. The atmosphere is different.

Everything seems to be different, except the God we all pretend to love. For He didn't make us different – some black, some white, some tall, some fat, some young, some old – to divide us, but to unite us.

Those differences were supposed to be constant reminders that we all have a part to play, that on some days a leader would lead and on others follow. That the carpenter would build and the painter brighten. That the engineer would construct and the designer decorate.

That the singer would sing, the sweeper would sweep, the faithful would keep us all on track.
That we'd all seek out our divine call and fulfill it.
But the images and differences that have become idols are keeping many from their call, keeping many out of churches

that will help them find it because the places of worship they have searched for fit their preconceived beliefs, but not God's divine plan.

There are white people walking around unsaved because the black preacher God has called to touch him pretend not to know him. He's not black like me, so I can't relate, he's thinking.

There are black people walking around lost because the white preacher and parishioner called to witness to them are hiding behind the false notion that they don't understand his "culture."

I resented Jesus because I was hiding behind that false logic, that God made some black and others white to separate us, not strengthen us.

The Hardest Piece
I've Ever Written

WHEN YOU HAVE FINISHED THIS, you would have read the hardest piece I've ever written. Many times, fear has forced my fingers away from the keyboard.

For I, too, have felt that certain fear we rarely talk about and almost never admit feeling: the fear of black men. Yes, despite my 6'0" 220 pound frame. Despite my college football background.

Despite my growing up with eight brothers – black brothers – and attending an almost all-black high school.

Despite my black skin.

I've felt myself brace, tense up, when walking down a sidewalk toward a group of folks that look like me.
I've heard myself think, heard myself say, things that suggest those vile, racist stereotypes reside in me.

In me, despite my God-fearing foundation.

When I watch the evening news and see a black man accused of a crime, I cringe. But there is no surprise in my eyes.

For when I close them and think of criminal, I see black and male.

Someone who looks like me.

I've learned racism springs from somewhere other than our rational mind.

When you have finished this, you would have read the hardest piece I've ever written, for it's hard to admit one's shortcomings, hard to stand up on a stage and tell you that

I'm just like you. Hard to accept the irony of the images that haunt me and chase me, knowing others have crossed the road to avoid my dark presence, followed my every move in and out of stores, looked straight through me, never noticing I was – I am.

But I must tell you, for it's the only way I know to get your attention. The only way to help you move past the fear that have kept so many mired in a cloud of confusion and irrational thought.

For I know where the irrational has been birthed. Right there in the percentages – almost 70 percent of South Carolina inmates are black, about 45 percent nationwide – and the images.

Seldom, though, do we question how the image of me affects those who must judge me.

I know of what I speak. My oldest brother is a convicted murdered. A high school friend is blind from a gunshot wound to the head, shot by others who look like us. Other high school friends went to prison for armed robbery and car jacking.

A student I once tutored is dead from the bullet of a police officer, an officer he shot and killed a split second earlier, their bullets apparently passing in other in the air.

All black. All male. Every one.

I've seen the ugliness that can make us forget there is so much beauty. The beauty of my brothers proudly raising their sons and daughters and respecting their wives. The beauty of the many black men who work in ties and three-piece suits, or aprons and McDonald's hats, to provide for families they love.

When you have finished reading this, you would have read the hardest piece I've ever written, for there's no logical way to explain away fact. Facts we've grown too accustomed to citing, too lazy to examine.

For what do they say about me, and the nine out of 10

black males who never commit violent crimes or the roughly eight of 10 who never see the inside of a courtroom as a defendant.

What do they say about the studies that show that when income and educational levels are factored in, there is no statistical difference in violence levels between blacks and whites.

What do they say about the man you – me – greeted last night with suspicion, when all he was ready to return was a smile. A gentle glance.

What does it say about us, all of us, who dare demand justice and equality and fairness, but dare not examine subconscious forces that stand in the way for fear of being labeled something that we are: flawed human beings who sometimes make irrational, snap judgments.

It says absolutely nothing.

Yet, all too much.

I Never Thanked the Slaves

I NEVER THANKED THE SLAVES. Been too busy being ashamed. Ashamed of their dark, black, dry skin. Crusted bare toes. The shackles on their feet. Their kinky hair. Their seeming acceptance of a life full of hell here on earth.

For too long, I've been blinded by the shame.

For years, I wrapped it up in anger. Focused on the rapes and the Middle Passage dipped in blood and the lashings on the backs and the stolen mothers and sold fathers and feet dangling in mid-air and the long days in the sun. Cursed those slave owners armed with rifles and leather whips, prayed they had become Satan's guests.

But I never thanked the slaves.
It's as if all I've ever seen, all they've ever been to me, were pieces of a dreaded history I longed to forget ... wished never existed.

The dirty looks I've dealt with in my short life, I inadvertently placed at the feet of my ancestors.

Ancestors, I dare admit, I once loathed for being fragile and feebleminded.

I hated them, I really did, because I thought they were weak.

Dumb.

In between trips to the movie theater or mall, I have thumped my chest, proclaimed my strength, and assured others I would never have succumbed to the chains and ropes that held the slaves captive.

Reacting to the security guard following me in the department store, I have cried about the horrible conditions black men have to endure in an unforgiving America, then patted myself on the back for how I had overcome. In classrooms, I screamed because their faces never showed up in my history books while silently praying ... hoping I'd never have to discuss their plight in the presence of my white classmates.

For if they saw them, they'd see me, too, see my fear, disgust for a skin I pretended to love. But I never thanked the slaves, been to busy denying that my shortcomings were my own. Never sent up a prayer, never needed their spirits to hear my call, begging their forgiveness.

For I had been an ungrateful son, looking past their tortured souls, their strength, their faith, and instead proudly claimed the kings and queens of an Africa I've never known.

But ungrateful no longer, today I shout to the heavens with pride, thanking them for a life well lived.

Though they were shackled, their spirits soared.

They were beaten, sometimes to death, but never did they become lifeless.

Their long voyage of suffering and death has ended in me living in this land of opportunity. But make no mistake, no slave trader deserves that credit, only the amount Judas deserves for the Resurrection.

It was the will of the slave that has given me life.

For they were great. Beautiful. Wise. Fragile. Loved. Weak. Wonderful. Ugly.

They were me before I was.

Today, though I step out of my shame, I can't go back and nurse their wounds from horsewhips or dry their tears.

All I can do is live a life of freedom, anchored by the strength passed on through generations, filled with a spirit that could never die.

I will never succumb to the superficial shackles of today that could dim my tomorrow.

For I am the hope of the slave.

Lesson From A Little Boy

IT'S 18 YEARS LATER, and I still wonder about the little boy I never met. I don't know his name, first or last, don't know his age – though I believe he was about 10 – don't know what he has grown to become.

But I can still see him standing there, leaning against a small pole while Hell was trying to break loose all around him.

He was standing silently, a look of bewilderment dripping from his young cheeks, between a small group of adult Ku Klux Klan members and a growing, angry mob separated by an army of Charleston, S.C., police.

I was a member of the angry mob. He, of the Klan.

It was a Sunday morning during the summer of 1990. I was in town attending the S.C. Governor's School. The Klan was marching. And the boy was watching. I don't know what or who, exactly, but can imagine he watched us.

All of us.

The fair-skinned men and women on stage, dressed in green and white and dark colored robes and pointed tops on their heads. The dark- and fair-skinned men and women in the mob.

The man screaming white power from the stage, the woman showering him with animosity from the crowd.

The heavily armed police officers standing stern-faced.

He may have noticed me, with chest out, heart rate rising and anger boiling over.

Anger at what, I don't recall, for the Klan that day included about a dozen people; most looked malnourished, poor. They in no way resembled my vision of what they would be, what they were. An odd mixture of hate and curiosity pushed my legs forward that morning and carried me hurriedly from a morning church service to the march. The night before, I remembered the images of the lifeless bodies of black men dangling from ropes tied around tree branches. I remembered the dogs and water hoses. I remembered the burned crosses and stories of anguish and pain.

It was as if I'd dipped into a well and drank from our long history of hate, drank from it to ready myself for a battle that didn't need to be fought.

And I took it along with me to the march that Sunday morning, proud of my anger.

Until I saw him. He was standing there, in a pair of jeans, worn in places a little boy's jeans should wear away, from days spent on the monkey bars and on the playground and in ballgames and running through the woods and climbing trees and happily breaking bones through a carefree journey of young life.

But that Sunday morning, he was standing there looking out into the crowd without seeing, listening without hearing. His smile, his laughter, was nowhere to be found.

A large park with room enough for a little boy to run for days was just yards away.

But he couldn't see it.

We blocked his view.

All of us.

So he just stood against the pole. An eerie silence surrounded him in that sea of deafening hostility. I don't know what's become of him, don't know how many days he spent at the feet of family members – the ones who loved him and feed him and kept him safe – learning about hate. Don't know how many days he's reflected on those few hours from that morning, hours of hearing strange men and women hold in contempt his kind.

But I know what's become of my once simplistic view of what we call life, and love, and hate.

I threw it out that day and walked away ashamed of my righteous anger.

That little boy I never met taught me those feelings were useless. Taught me they were limiting, not liberating. I wonder what I taught him.

How Do We Distribute Payment For Suffering

NO ONE CAN TRULY argue that the victims shouldn't be compensated for a tragedy that has affected us in ways in which we're still coming to grips. It destroyed families, shook long-held beliefs of justice, and forever changed the way we live and view each other. Though their loss can never be measured in dollars, they deserve compensation.

Compensation for seeing the lives of their loved ones snuffed out, for their pain and suffering.

Compensation for all the years the families have been robbed of invaluable earning potential.

There is little doubt, then, that black Americans should be paid reparations for the holocaust that was slavery. The only question is how to distribute the funds.

Those are among the arguments that have been made by legal and scholarly stalwarts (the now late) Johnnie Cochran Jr., Randall Robinson, Cornel West and others who want to sue the federal government for trillions of dollars for what they believe is long overdue comeuppance for black suffering. The Bush Administration and Congress became unlikely allies in their cause. The much discussed fund for the victim's of Sept. 11 – which compensated even those not directly hurt by that day's event – is be Exhibit A.

Each of the arguments made to justify the Sept. 11 fund can be used to legitimize the fight for reparations.

And furthermore, the argument is strengthened when

you consider it was our government – not Osama bin Laden and 19 crazed hijackers – most responsible.

Reparations proponents can play an intriguing game of point-counterpoint:

Point: Black people have been receiving reparations in the form of affirmative action and other social programs for decades.

Counterpoint: Americans raised $1.5 billion for victims of Sept. 11. Children who lost a parent were promised free education for as long as they live. Insurance companies honored policies that didn't even cover terrorism. That doesn't include the pensions, Social Security and other retirement funds many collected.

Point: I had nothing to do with slavery and shouldn't be made to pay for it.

Counterpoint: You had nothing to do with the Sept. 11 attacks but your money was used to pay the families. There is nothing untoward about us all paying the bill when government screws up, particularly when it openly and willingly participates in one of Earth's greatest evils.

Point: It would be impossible to figure out who deserved what.

Counterpoint: That didn't stop Washington lawyer Kenneth Feinberg from calculating a dead person's lost earning potential.

Point: Congress only approved the fund in an attempt to save the airline industry from the billions it stood to lose in court battles.

Counterpoint: The country stands to lose trillions if the reparations group wins.

Point: 3,000 people lost mothers, fathers, husbands, wives, sons and daughters Sept. 11, and thousands of others were maimed and wounded. You shouldn't belittle their pain.

Counterpoint: Several million over four centuries lost their lives during the Middle Passage and slavery.

Millions were beaten, robbed and raped. Countless families were ripped apart. Millions followed them and faced another century of lynchings, Jim Crow and daily terrorism that, on many days, saw law enforcement turn a blind eye or help in the flogging. A de facto slavery lasted in the South up until World War II, whereby black men were arrested and imprisoned on trumped-up charges then ``loaned'' to companies such as U.S. Steel. And we are still fighting flawed philosophies and social systems that were cemented in that era.

I, for one, disagree with both reparations and the Sept. 11 fund. There are countless events in history that have had a negative impact on us all, and it's impractical to repay our loss with money.

Our country in too many instances has proved itself hypocritical, though, recognizing the pain of some while ignoring the suffering of others.
I can't help but find it fascinating that Americans were willing to spend billions to make right something someone else made wrong but resist something as simple as an apology for our country's own misdeeds.

Flawed Leaders
and Symbols

Jackson Deserves Spot in History

THERE IS DEATH.

There are taxes.

And there is the heap of praise I receive from some white readers every time I disagree with the likes of the Rev. Jesse Jackson. (To a much smaller extent, I get the dreaded "Uncle Tom" label from a handful of black readers at the same time.)

They seem to say it's OK, welcome even, when I write about race from an angle that assuages their preconceived notions, but never in the opposite direction.

It's a curious reality, one I've long noticed but little noted. I'll note it today. Jackson and others have problems and are as flawed as the rest of us. Which leader isn't? And I believe they too often waste invaluable political capital standing up for causes that really aren't worthy.

Jackson led a march to get Don Imus fired, this decades after marching in a movement that helped stop blacks from being publicly lynched and discriminated against in a variety of ways. Nothing better illustrates the devolution of the Civil Rights movement.

But I will never have the kind of disdain for him that many white readers seem to, for one simple reason.

He was there.

He was there when it mattered the most. When plenty of white ministers and whites in general and too many middle-class blacks pleaded for calm and had a wait-until-never attitude about forcing this country to live out its true ideals, Jackson and others like him were there, on the front lines, pushing down barriers and setting precedent.

They were there when Martin Luther King Jr. was shot, when the dogs and the water hoses were turned loose. They were there.

That doesn't give them carte blanche or absolution from personal failings or the right to insist the younger generation march in lockstep. I don't have to deny their imperfections to understand what they will always represent. Before you pretend that you can't, think about some of this country's most influential figures.

Thomas Jefferson said all men were created equal yet owned slaves. Confederate flag wavers deny slavery's role in the Civil War, even though it was precisely for that reason they seceded.

Conservatives love Ronald Reagan unconditionally and call Jackson a race hustler. They have forgotten how Reagan used race baiting to kick off his presidential campaign by pandering to racist whites and handled the South African apartheid regime in questionable ways.

I'll disagree with Jackson in this space again and point out when he goes wrong. But I'll never forget that it was because of people like him that I have this space at all.

Remember Leader's Message

I CRANKED UP THE GAS-POWERED Lowe's power washer, aimed the hose toward my wife's car and sprayed.

It was a Sunday afternoon, and since I was washing her car for the first time in months, I pulled out the power washer. It had been sitting in the garage for months since the two times I used it to clean a house we were selling.

The kids climbed inside the Jeep, hoping to see the water beat against the windows. I marveled at their excitement over such an insignificant event, about how water bouncing off glass could bring smiles to those who have brought me so much joy.

My attention waned for a split second and my right pinky slipped into the flow of the powerful stream of water. It hurt so bad I thought it had been ripped off. It was bloodied and bruised. I thought about it the next day while standing at Myrtle Beach City Hall listening to a string of speakers reflect on Martin Luther King Jr. Day.

If a split-second encounter with a high-flow stream of water can cause that much damage, how much damage was incurred by those who faced the police dogs and water hoses in their fight for equality?

And I wondered if I should be proud to live in a country in which someone like me can own a house, car and power washer and pursue my dreams, or saddened that many before me were denied the chance to do so because they had the hue of skin I inherited. Or both.

Then I thought about how my life changed when my kids were born, about how much of the time and energy I once used to volunteer in schools and mentor teenagers shifted to trying to provide my kids with a stable life, about how my wife and I have discussed, but not figured out how to establish the proper balance between how we once lived and how we currently do.

"We gotta get back to being the extended family we were before the civil rights [movement]," speaker Dr. Covia Stanley said during Monday's rally on city hall's steps. ``We have become a selfish people. We don't think about helping others.''

Speaker Abdullah Mustafa of the Conway branch of the National Association for the Advancement of Colored People asked if we are truly walking in King's reflection.

"The key is, what have we done to make our condition better?" Abdullah asked. ``What have we done to help others?''

King said everyone can be great because everyone can serve. Martin Luther King Jr. Day has passed. But that message shouldn't be forgotten.

Talk About Race Causes Uneasiness

THE REV. KYLON MIDDLETON stood before an audience of mostly black students during a Black History Month program at Carvers Bay High School and said that "black is beautiful" and "it's good to be black in America" and briefly mentioned "black power." The black students excitedly reacted, forcing Middleton to calm them.

"This does not negate any other heritage," he went on to say, "be it Anglo or Saxon... be it Judeo or Christian... if you are from German descent or rather from Italian descent. This does not negate you, but don't hate on us because we are glad to be black."

He spoke about a character from Toni Morrison's "Bluest Eye," a young girl who longed to be white because "during that time being white meant being right."

"Being blond hair and having blue eyes meant that you were beautiful," Middleton explained. "But I come to Carvers Bay High with my nappy hair and my wide nose and my big lips. Although your hips may be wide, although your nose may be broad, you can look in the mirror and say that you are beautiful because you are a black person."

Middleton did nothing wrong. His speech was designed to uplift, yet the white students and their parents who were bothered by what he said had every right to feel uncomfortable, even offended.

Such is the strange reality and complexity of race. It doesn't allow us to pretend that there's only one way to speak about the subject and one way to hear it, no matter how much we want to.

Isn't it ironic that the Georgetown County school board may be forced to gerrymander its elections to assure a black candidate can win office in the same year Sen. Barack Obama has proven that white people, by the millions, will vote for a black candidate they like – even without a specially designed voting district? Our truncated views of the country's racial history also color our racial outlook.

"Black power" to the uninitiated may sound like ``white power'' in reverse. But the latter was made famous by the Ku Klux Klan, who terrorized and lynched black people; the former was made famous by Tommie Smith and John Carlos during the 1968 Olympics. The two sprinters, with bowed heads and black-gloved fists, used it as a form of nonviolent protest. And singer James Brown sang ``I'm Black and I'm Proud'' before diverse crowds.

That was then. Expecting a white high school student in 2008 to feel comfortable in a mostly black assembly while listening to ``black power'' is asking a lot. That doesn't mean we should base what's acceptable to say on who might be offended. We shouldn't.

But there is an imbalance.

Such assemblies give the perception that's it's OK for white students to be offended in the name of uplifting black students even while many schools throughout the state frown upon black students being offended by sentiment and symbols that carry historical significance for some white students, such as the Confederate flag.

The black power chant was mostly designed to create black unity in a world hostile to civil rights but also used by some of the most militant segments of the Civil Rights Movement. The same can be said of the Confederate flag. It has been used by the Ku Klux Klan but some whites can legitimately claim that it is about heritage. Not every

Confederate soldier fought to prolong slavery or owned slaves.

I don't mind that the Rev. Middleton spoke or even that some were offended even while I question the continued usefulness of such assemblies. Students should occasionally feel uncomfortable, challenged. Hiding them from the messiness of life benefits no one. Schools are ideally suited to help them navigate that messiness.

But in the quest to end discrimination against blacks, too often we don't seem to mind when we marginalize whites.

That must change.

Feels Like a Referendum on Blacks

IT FEELS LIKE a referendum on black people.

I know a vote against Barack Obama isn't a vote against black people and doesn't make a person racist.

I know November's election will be won or lost on the strength of the Obama and John McCain campaigns, their ability to dodge and weave, to punch and counterpunch, in the country's most intriguing contact sport. I know character issues and judgment, experience and ideology, and the candidates' positions will help voters decide upon whom to support.

I know it's not a referendum on black people. But it still feels like one.

Every time someone, like Geraldine Ferraro, says Obama is successful because of his race, it feels like they are saying it about me, about us, because we've heard it many times, no matter how hard we've worked, no matter how many obstacles we've overcome.

Every time someone refuses to shake his hand, like that older white gentlemen in Indiana during the primaries, and calls him unpatriotic, it feels like he is doing that to me, to us, because so many times it has happened, and we've mostly held our tongues to avoid being labeled angry and black, an unacceptable combination.

Every time someone says his wife isn't patriotic – because she dared to air her conflicted views about a country that had, for too many years, treated dark skin like a disease

– it feels like it is being said about me, about us.
Every time Obama has to answer for the Rev.
Jeremiah Wright and his racialized anger while McCain can
proclaim his loyalty to Ronald Reagan while not having to
answer for Reagan's racial misjudgments, it feels like that
double standard is being applied to me, to us. Because it
always has.

Reagan began his presidential campaign at a county
fair of white racists in Philadelphia, Miss., gave a pass to
South African Apartheid and helped perpetuate the myth of
``Cadillac welfare queens.'' He rolled back civil rights like no
president since.

He's the man McCain says he wants to emulate. And
no one calls him on it. No one bats an eye. No one conducts
a poll asking if Americans believe McCain shares Reagan's
views on race the way they still ask if Obama shares Rev.
Wright's.

I know it isn't. But it feels like a referendum on black
people.

Maybe that feeling is based on my own shortcomings
– or on the shortcomings of the country Obama and I love
anyway.

'Kooky' Claim Rooted in History

ONE COMMENT BY the Rev. Jeremiah Wright caught my attention more than the others because some have called it "just plain kooky."

"The government lied about inventing the HIV virus as a means of genocide against people of color," Wright said. While he was clearly wrong, the belief that spurred the comment isn't simply conspiratorial:

During the 40-year Tuskegee Syphilis Experiment, which lasted from 1932 to 1972, researchers studied the effects of syphilis by targeting rural Macon County in Alabama. About 400 black men, who were told they would receive free medical help from the U.S. Public Health Service, were never told they had the disease and were kept from treatment.

"By the time the study was exposed in 1972, 28 men had died of syphilis, 100 others were dead of related complications, at least 40 wives had been infected and 19 children had contracted the disease at birth," according to CNN.

In the 1980s and 1990s, the government allowed the testing of AIDS drugs on foster children (including those in North Carolina) who were poor and mostly minority, without providing basic protections to determine if the tests were worth the risk, an Associated Press analysis found. Researchers said it was the only way to provide at-risk kids with high-tech drugs, while others said it was akin to using them as guinea pigs.

According to a book review of "Medical Apartheid," the U.S. Army and CIA in the early 1950s exposed black Floridians to swarms of mosquitoes carrying yellow fever; black inmates in Philadelphia were used as research subjects to test pharmaceuticals; in the 1960s and '70s, black boys were subjected to sometimes paralyzing neurosurgery by a researcher who thought brain pathology caused hyperactive behavior; and in the 1990s, "African American youths in New York were injected with Fenfluramine – half of the deadly, discontinued weight loss drug Fen-Phen – by Columbia researchers investigating a hypothesis about the genetic origins of violence."

The CIA in 1998 acknowledged it had covered up Contra drug trafficking, a move that contributed to the crack epidemic.

This country has made amends for a lot. We've come a long way. That should never be forgotten.

But there is much to be learned from one man's angry, wrong-headed rantings – and from the history he is likely basing them on.

Democrats Still Have Shared Cause

I'M PROUD.

And I'm not ashamed to be proud. I'm proud that a man with dark skin, the color of which has held so many back for so long in our 232-year history, will head a major party presidential ticket.

That's why I can empathize with staunch supporters of Sen. Hillary Clinton.

I understand their disappointment.

They could sense something historic as well.

They wanted to smash through what Clinton called the "highest, hardest" glass ceiling, too, to prove that more than one demographic group can produce leaders capable of leading this nation.

But while we became fixated on making history, we forget our history.

We forgot that this kind of contest played itself out before, in the years right after the Civil War.

There were discussions about allowing former slaves to vote. But it devolved into a contest between blacks and women.

Some women were accused of trying to block black progress by protesting the 15th Amendment until women would also be given the right to vote. The esteemed Frederick Douglass was accused by esteemed women's advocates such as Elizabeth Cady Stanton of overlooking women's rights.

Two worthy causes, two justified views became a

muddled "me first," "me, too" argument. The rift healed, and they helped each other secure voting rights but not before giving in to their lower angels.

The same has happened this year. Clinton and Sen. Barack Obama were celebrated. They both are lawyers from prestigious universities. They both forfeited early fortune in service of their country, she with the Children's Defense Fund, and he as a low-paid community organizer on the streets of Chicago.

They both had fortuitous ascensions into the U.S. Senate, she after having her toughest challenger, Rudy Giuliani, diagnosed with prostate cancer, he after having his most formidable rival succumb to scandal.

They both were fortunate because women and blacks attaining high office in this country is rare. There are only 16 women U.S. senators in a country that's 51 percent female. But that's more than three times as many blacks that have served in the Senate in our history. Obama is the only current black senator.

We watched them easily outpace more experienced white men who had more foreign policy expertise, such as Sen. Joe Biden, in the presidential primary.

We watched them be treated fairly, sometimes unfairly, as they struggled with perceptions and questions about race and gender their all-white male Republican counterparts never had to face.

We watched them be brilliant, with Clinton's early fund-raising records and command of policy and Obama's speeches and command of caucuses.

We watched them be trite, with Clinton's tall tales about Bosnia and Obama's bitter comments about rural America.

We watched them be typical politicians, taking advantage of every gaffe and misstatement made by the other.

And we watched as their supporters talked up who

had it worse. Clinton's supporters reminded us that women didn't get the vote until 1920, a half century after blacks. Obama's countered that blacks only technically had the right since 1968, when all the poll taxes, rigged literacy tests and the Klan were finally overcome.

Neither of them mentioned that American Indians didn't achieve universal suffrage until 1957 and still have a steeper climb to the White House.

Nor did they mention that having a woman or black in the Oval Office, while significant, is largely symbolic in comparison to the right to vote, particularly given the challenges both groups continue to face. And we'll watch through November, wondering if Clinton and Obama will re-remember their common cause, like Douglass and Stanton eventually did, or become the primary barrier to each other's long-hoped-for success.

Don't Ignore Lott's Remarks

I WAS SITTING at the dinner table one night at a friend's. We were shooting the breeze, talking loudly, mostly about nothing. We laughed about how a dog psychic could lead O.J. to the real killers and light-heartedly, but half-seriously, talked about how the pastor was wrong for urging members of an area church to vote Tuesday – for all the Democrats on the ballot.

And that's when the 62-year-old pecan-colored woman at the table stopped laughing and turned deadly serious.

She turned to one of her nieces, her eyes steadying themselves like a fighter pilot locking on a target, and gave these words of warning:

"If I find out you vote Republican, I will slap the shit out of you!"

There was no joy in her voice, no, "I'm just kidding." She hadn't been much a part of the conversation before those words, wasn't much of a participant afterwards, but I shook as she shared her brief statement.

Her words threw me and the mix of young and old people sitting around that table, all of whom happen to be black.

It threw me because I'd never seen this woman angry, never heard her voice raised until that moment. And it threw me because I was a 20-something-year-old man who has prided himself on being choosey about the candidates for which he voted. Those candidates have included as many Republicans as Democrats.

For the longest time, I dismissed her words. Sort of let them fade from my brain as though they never existed, until the dust up with Sen. Trent Lott. His words at Strom Thurmond's 100th birthday party reminded me of her words and how I was foolish to ignore them and how foolish Republicans, or any American with a conscience, would be to ignore Lott's. Because they weren't a one-time slip of the tongue but rather confirmation of his seemingly life-long held beliefs.

Yet, it should be the country's, not Lott's, failure on trial. We've failed miserably, black and white Americans alike, on the issue of race because we thought a series of laws and social programs and the collection of racial data alone could overcome our past.

I was foolish to ignore that 62-year-old woman's words because they spoke to a pain that I, having grown up after most of the civil rights struggles, can only intellectualize. She grew up in an era when millions of Americans took pride in being racist, when a public lynching was a real threat. She grew up under government-sanctioned, public-supported bigotry.

She was a little girl trying to understand the world when Thurmond said nothing would make Negroes acceptable. She was a teenager when he performed the longest filibuster in U.S. history against civil rights legislation.

She was a young adult, trying to make her way, even as doors slammed in her face for no other reason than her having been born the wrong color, when the Republican party, and many Democrats, began playing upon racism to court votes. And she was a gray-haired old lady with creaky knees when Lott reminder her of it all.

Thurmond and others like him may have eventually

walked away from the hateful venom they so effectively spewed, but it doesn't mean their repentance removed all the scars they inflicted.

As we count the many ways we've moved forward in this country, the way Jim Crow, the official version anyway, has long since been killed. As we orgasmicly outline how the black middle class has grown and black Americans are the wealthiest, healthiest and most educated dark-skinned people the world has ever seen ... we'd better stop acting as though that 62-year-old woman is dead, that she isn't entitled to her anger – her rage – particularly when every time she expresses it she's either ignored or shooed away like an annoying fly, or told her pain – her life – shouldn't be discussed outside of history classes.

We must find a way to stop ignoring her pain while remembering to not become blinded by it.

'Plantation' Carries Area's Loaded Past Into Present

AS HERB THOMPSON AND HIS WIFE drove through the entrance of a community to tour a home they saw in a newspaper ad, something caught their eye.

It said Cimerron Plantation.

"I ain't living on no damn plantation," Thompson told his wife.

Such reactions have marketers and some developers reconsidering the wisdom of using "plantation" to name communities.

The Litchfield Co. and Burroughs & Chapin Co. Inc., two of the Myrtle Beach area's longest-standing and most influential real estate companies, won't use the word again unless a new development has ties to a historical plantation.

Even a bank, Plantation Federal, is considering a name change after 21 years. The word means elegance to some but represents pain and suffering for others. Both views are rooted in history – but each is incomplete without the other.

"There has been an explosion in sensitivity to language," said Edna Andrews, a Duke University professor of linguistics and Slavic studies. "Certain words are reminiscent of certain historical periods and become quite controversial. ... Meanings change." Almost 1,300 incorporated businesses in the state – including 182 along the Grand Strand – have "plantation" in their title, according to the S.C. secretary of state.

About 70 developments on the Multiple Listing Service, which covers most of the Grand Strand and parts of Brunswick County, N.C., are named "plantation" because the word has helped drive home sales. Many of those developments don't have ties to the area's more than 200 historic plantations.

"[Our] new homes team does avoid the use of 'plantation' because they believe that it does not really carry the same marketing weight that it used to ... and the word does impact some people in a negative way," said B&C spokesman Pat Dowling, who is white.

The development-as-plantation phenomenon is part of the country's conflicted racial legacy. Look no further than the dollar bill for an example. On it is emblazoned the image of George Washington, the nation's first president, an undisputed American hero who helped usher in freedom – and a slave owner.

"The word 'plantation' has almost become synonymous for 'estate' the way [developers] use it, except those who are trying to bring out the history of the place," said Horry County historian Ben Burroughs.
Marketers and developers choose names and images that might connect with a potential buyer on an emotional level. When it comes to "plantation," it works – in ways that are intended and in ways that aren't.

"For the current generation of African-Americans who live in areas [where their relatives were slaves] – to the degree that there is what I call 'a historic memory' – it is one of oppression and denial of basic human rights. It suggests privilege for one group and denial of them for the other," said William Falk, a professor of sociology at the University of Maryland. He has written extensively on the American South, including a book situated in the Lowcountry. He is working on a project examining the evolving plantation and changing demography and economic development in the

Lowcountry.

"I do not believe that any developer – in the Southwest or elsewhere where Native Americans live – has re-introduced to the language the term 'reservation' and then made it fashionable as a residential development," Falk said.

For the Thompsons, who are black, "plantation" conjures up images of the hit TV mini-series "Roots." They see mass murder and hungry sharks swimming behind ships in water stained red by the bodies of slaves thrown overboard. They said that they're sensitive for the same reasons many in the Jewish community are sensitive to reminders of the Holocaust.

"Would Cimerron Concentration Camp be OK?" Thompson asked.

But Thompson, the facilities coordinator for the campus recreation program at Coastal Carolina University and a graduate of historically black Howard University, said once the initial shock subsided, they took a tour of the home – and loved it.

That was 17 years ago. The Thompsons still call Cimerron Plantation home.

Sort of.

They almost didn't buy because of the name, but have stayed because of the neighbors – many of whom are white. It's the one place where they've experienced no overt discrimination, something Herb Thompson faced plenty of growing up in Clinton in the 1960s.

Even so, they tell visitors they live at Cimerron development, not Cimerron Plantation.

Thompson has told his son not to linger on the country's painful racial past, the same lesson his parents taught him. His home is decorated with African artifacts because, while he doesn't want to dwell on the past, he doesn't want to forget either.

"What our people went through on the plantation,

why do you still refer to them as "plantation?" Thompson asks of the newest developments. Cimerron was named about 25 years ago. Others said they didn't pay attention to the name or see it as a sign of progress that black people could own homes in any neighborhood of their choosing.

A hodgepodge of feelings was evident among white people interviewed, as well. Jim Vallos is a 36-year-old white man from Ohio. He owns three condos in River Oaks Plantation.

"Plantation" makes him think of "nothing more than a lot of land for crop-growing."

"The name of our development had no effect on my decision to buy there," he said. Developers said, for their target audience, the word "plantation" has long conjured up images of "Gone With the Wind" and the mystique of white-columned homes on large estates.

"We added 'plantation' to the name to help portray the grandness of this property and add to the island resort nature of the community," said Matt Scalise, the broker-in-charge for North Beach Plantation oceanfront complex that is home to some of the area's most expensive condos. "In essence, our goal is to create a destination location and to brand North Beach as a luxury getaway as well as an upscale residential community with a relaxed island attitude," said Scalise, who is white.

The meaning of "plantation" is as multifaceted as the country's racial history. "Although slavery was a horrible thing, I did not equate a Southern plantation with only slavery," said Barbara Graham, a 36-year-old white woman from Little River. "The vision of the word 'plantation' really was molded in my brain as some sort of beautiful place as seen in many old movies.

"The visual is always the columned homes and tons of azaleas and droopy, old oak trees with Spanish moss. ... I never thought there was a dark side to the use of that word. If there is, that makes me sad."

Jamie Northrup, 50, grew up in northwest Ohio. She's white.

"It does conjure up visions of white, upper-class people treating other people poorly," she said. "It amazes me that, in 2007, housing developments are continuing to be named with 'plantation.'"Coastal Carolina University professor Preston McKever-Floyd sees nothing wrong with developers using the term.

McKever-Floyd was one of the first black students to attend Conway High School during the area's first attempts at integrating schools. There were no dogs or water hoses or elected officials greeting McKever-Floyd at the schoolhouse door, as happened in other Southern cities during the civil rights movement.

"I know that there are still actual historical plantations and the word itself is neutral," he said. "It is such a part of this Lowcountry history. As a result, I don't find it offensive."

Johnie Rivers, a longtime volunteer for the S.C. Historical Society, has identified 14 authentic Horry County plantations on her Web site, which lists more than 2,000 S.C. plantations, including more than 200 in Georgetown County.

Her definition? A large farm on which most of the work was done by slaves. In Georgetown County, that often meant rice plantations.

In Horry County, indigo and other less lucrative plants were more the norm. Crops such as potatoes, cotton and most others used for food and profit are also part of the area's heritage.

The area was littered with other kinds of plantations as well, including those that had no slaves. Some farmers used the term to denote a large estate.

Webster's New World College Dictionary makes no mention of slaves in its definitions, which include "a colony or new settlement" or "an estate cultivated by workers living on it." The area's "plantations" are not all alike and include some of the country's oldest.

There are gated plantation developments with multimillion-dollar homes and those with homes that are valued at less than Horry County's $210,000 median home price. Visitors marvel at the statues at Brookgreen Gardens in Pawleys Island, which was once Brookgreen Plantation and three others. Golfers take tee shots over preserved slave cemeteries on the former plantation that is known as the Heritage Club. In 1860, more than 60 slaves worked on the 3,194-acre Ark Plantation where Surfside Beach leaders and businesses today fight over smoking bans and host annual family fests.

Hopsewee just off U.S. 17 in southern Georgetown County has been preserved since it was established about 40 years before the American Revolution. It was home to the only father-and-son combination to serve the Continental Congress, Thomas Lynch Jr. and his father. Thomas Lynch Jr. was also a signer of the Declaration of Independence.

It was home to hundreds of slaves who toiled from dusk to dawn for four years to clear a swampy area infested with insects, snakes and alligators to make way for rice fields that made their owners among the country's wealthiest. True Blue in Pawleys Island was one of the more than 200 authentic Georgetown plantations listed on south-carolina-plantations.com. It has a golf course and country club today.

Developers are partnering with archaeologists to develop 18th-century Beneventum Plantation on the Black River.

The plantation's formal gardens will be re-created through research and archaeology, as well as the plantation's house, which was built between 1746 and 1756. Homes costing between $200,000 to $600,000 were planned for the development's first phase.

Then there are plantations such as Windsor in the

Surfside Beach area. Realtors said it has no historical ties. It was named by a Nations Homes executive.

Bennie Swans said he can't forget that history.

Swans, who helped secure official recognition of Martin Luther King Jr. Day in Myrtle Beach and pushed for a larger minority presence in government contracts, put a deposit on a house in Wedgefield Plantation.

Wedgefield includes a variety of home styles, tennis courts, numerous live oaks and a golf course. A former slave house faces a pool house. It is owned by a friend of Swans', a white developer who purchased it about a year ago. That developer is helping Swans establish a prison rehabilitation program.

"Good white folks who don't mean no harm just don't see the relevance of it," Swans said. "They simply have no concept of the pain and suffering, about what 'plantation' means."

Swans, who is black, walked away from what he said was "the best property at the best price and in the best condition" of all those he toured.
He has no problem with other people buying into a plantation development, just that "I couldn't deal with it."

"My wife said to me, 'You are out of your mind,'" Swans said. "I could not, in good conscience, live on a plantation. That is as offensive to me as the Confederate flag. We entertain people; we have grandchildren. How could we justify living in a big house on a plantation, given the history?"

That Wedgefield house was purchased by Seymour Brinbaum, a Jewish man who said his parents left slavery in Russia. Brinbaum said he understood Swans' feelings but laughingly told him it wasn't too late to buy a lot near the home he passed on. The lot's value has more than tripled in four years.

"Words are very funny things," he said. "History changes everything."

Obama

Racial Hyprocrisy Too Common

WE ARE A NATION OF RACIAL HYPOCRITES. Not one of us would pass the kind of racial purity test many are applying to Barack Obama.

Not those who voted to re-elect Rep. Thad Viers after he was caught on tape using multiple racial epithets during an ugly domestic dispute, nor those who plan to vote for him in November.

Not those who hold uncritical views of Ronald Reagan, even though his administration had a too-cozy relationship with the apartheid regime in South Africa and was credited with dismantling numerous civil rights protections.

Not those who look the other way when the likes of Pat Robertson and Jerry Falwell make incendiary remarks about race or blame America for the Sept. 11 terrorist attacks. (Notice how Robertson and Falwell could say such things without being labeled anti-American.)

Not those who are angry that Gov. Mark Sanford forced two leaders of the S.C. Highway Patrol to resign after they did little to punish a trooper who used nigger while threatening to shoot a black motorist, unless they believe it's OK to remain supportive of that trooper but not OK that Obama refused to completely distance himself from his pastor while denouncing his pastor's comments.

Not those who wanted Don Imus fired for his racially-tinged comments but excuse the language used by black rappers and entertainers and the past racially-divisive comments of the Rev. Jesse Jackson and the Rev. Al Sharpton.

Not those who use Mark Fuhrman as a guest commentator, knowing his lies about his frequent use of the word nigger helped sink the prosecution's case in the racially-charged O.J. Simpson trial.

Not those who have been silent on Sen. John McCain's embrace of Bob Jones University, his double talk about the Confederate flag and his acceptance of an endorsement by the fire-breathing Rev. John Hagee.

Not those who have uncomfortably laughed while a friend or a neighbor or a parent made racist jokes and loved them anyway. Not those who would be appalled if there was a movement to remove George Washington's face from the dollar bill, even though Washington was one of the nation's most prominent slaveowners.

This country is soaked in racial contradiction. Every ethnic group is in on the act.

Each of us has embraced someone who has said or done racist things because each of us recognizes that people are complex than their worst acts.

Racial hypocrites deny that reality.

Unfortunately, too many of us wear that label without realizing that we do.

Imperfection Plagues Us All

I'LL TRY TO TELL YOU this without sounding like an ungrateful, unpatriotic American.

Ungrateful I'm not. I live in the best country ever created, and haven't forgotten.

But I hate that the Founding Fathers were slave owners, hate that they sang the praises of God, fought against tyranny, were brave souls willing to give their lives for liberty... and beat, raped and murdered men, women and children because they were dark-skinned.

I hate that Abraham Lincoln is seen as a black savior, as if he didn't believe, didn't say, he was against the equality of the races, that whites should always be seen as superior. I hate that that came from a man who saved the country, a feat from which I daily benefit.

I hated finding out Martin Luther King Jr. was a philandering womanizer even as he helped lead this country to a better place, one where success isn't so black and white, but murky, more open to all.

I hate how we feel the need to sanitize, overlook ignore their failings because they accomplished great things.

If only it were so easy.

It strikes me as curious it's not.

For we despise Louis Farrakhan, are taken aback by his disparaging comments about gays and Jews. But he's the same leader who helped save thousands from crack-infested streets and preaches more about personal responsibility than hate.

I wonder why we do that. Why we compartmentalize, deeming some saints, others evil incarnate. Why we refuse to recognize they are or were living, breathing human beings, prone to weakness, physical and moral, short of perfection, like us all.

I wonder why it was hard for me to feel love for my two younger brothers when they moved in with my wife and me. They were out on bond and under house arrest awaiting trial for charges ranging from possession of crack cocaine and marijuana with intent to distribute to possessing an illegal firearm.

My parents' Chevrolet Blazer sat in the front yard, under a white tarp, full of bullet holes and windows shattered thanks to the handiwork of drive-by cowards gunning for my brothers.

I was angry as I stood before the judge, assuring her they weren't flight risks. Angrier still when, six days later, I drove them back to St. Stephen after they informed me they didn't want to follow my house rules, one saying he was man enough to go to jail, too old for other people's oppressive rules, and the other quietly agreeing.

I wonder why it was hard for me to look them in the eyes after that, harder still to continue praying daily they would grow up and walk God's path.

I wonder why I stole cookies from my parents' room when I was younger, change from their drawers. Why in high school I drove my father's truck 125 miles per hour down the highway, racing against friends, endangering my life and the lives of two 15-year-old passengers.

I wonder why I've considered myself a complete failure after mistakes, forgetting to notice successes.

And, further still, why I find it easy to forgive myself for walking a less than clean path through this life, while finding it sometimes impossible to extend God's love to others who haven't found perfection.

Obama and Me and Black Son

ON MAY 5, 2008, a dozen Philadelphia police officers were captured on tape kicking and beating three young black men. On May 7, the Rev. Al Sharpton and others were arrested in New York City while protesting the acquittal of police officers who killed an unarmed young black.

Sandwiched in between was the day Sen. Barack Obama won the North Carolina primary, all but wrapping up the Democratic presidential nomination and becoming the first black man to lead a major party ticket in our 232-year history. Those days made me think more about the challenge of raising my six-year-old black son.

Obama accepted the nomination on the 45th anniversary of Martin Luther King's : "I Have A Dream" speech at the March on Washington. That was 40 years after the Kerner Commission found "two Americas," one black, one white.

The events aren't connected, except in one significant way: perception.

The perception that Al Sharpton, and others like him, is too eager to blame racism for every societal shortcoming.

The perception that cops are too eager to ship black men off to a "prison industrial complex" that thrives on black dysfunction.

The perception that too many young black men are considered suspect for good reason, given that they are more likely to be killed by other young black men than by racist cops. Police chased down the men in Philadelphia after an alleged drug deal gone bad.

The perception that Obama's candidacy is long overdue in a country that was founded upon freedom and the exploitation of dark-skinned people. None of those perceptions lends themselves to easy analysis. Each of them is old. Except Obama. A black man just months away from the presidency is new.

I'm 35 years old and didn't expect to see it. Maybe that's why I feel more emotionally involved in presidential politics than I ever have.

Initially, Obama wasn't considered black enough because he didn't bear the scars of the dogs and water hoses. Neither do I. By the time I was born in South Carolina in 1972, the "Whites Only" signs had been removed.

Then it was unsettling for some that he garnered so many black votes, as though it was a crime for black people to vote for the first viable black presidential candidate after spending their entire adult lives voting for white men. I understood. Some said I wasn't mainstream enough to command space as the primary columnist for my newspaper, that I saw things through the black perspective too often, as if seeing the world through anything but my own eyes was possible.

Then he was considered out of touch because he had dark skin yet attended elite schools. So did I, graduating from Davidson College, one of the "New Ivies." Never mind that Obama had a single mother who had to use Food Stamps or that my family relied on government cheese and free school lunches.

Then he was considered too black because his pastor said offensive things, and because he initially refused to abandon the man who introduced him to Christ. I got that, too. I attended the Million Man March, which was organized by a black man who has uttered anti-Semitic comments. I went to see if black men could gather for a positive cause, a commitment to personal and social responsibility, given what I'd witnessed growing up – seeing a friend who was blinded by a bullet to the brain during a nightclub fight, a brother convicted of murder, a father who beat my mother. And I remain friends with a NAACP leader who spent decades angering and insulting the sensibilities of whites because I know he was always about more, about uplifting the poor and voiceless.

Then a white man disparaged Obama by calling the would-be-president "an unpatriotic Muslim" and wouldn't shake his hand. I won't forget the white man who refused to shake mine while I interviewed him, or the time a white reader said I was secretly flashing a gang sign in my column photo, or the anonymous writer who sends racial epithet-filled threatening letters, saying I got my position because I was black, just as Geraldine Ferraro said Obama was successful primarily because of his race, just as she claimed 24 years earlier about Jesse Jackson.

Then Lynn Westmoreland, a Republican representative from Georgia, called Obama "uppity." The following week a reader sent me a letter, signing it "Tom the Tinker." He did include a return address.

"I looked up the definition of 'UPPITY' in my dictionary and, guess what, it showed a picture of you," it read. "Take the 'race' chip off your shoulders and be a real man instead of a ward of the Federal Government."

But like Obama, I know those obstacles are few compared to my opportunities, those barriers not nearly as daunting as they must have been when Obama's pastor was growing up. I know that ugly is far out weighed by the good. Millions of white people line up to hear Obama speak and want him to be president. And while a few white readers call me nigger, the majority appreciates what I do.

And I understand, as Obama must, that his triumph, while seminal, isn't an elixir. Because while he could take the oath of office during the centennial of the NAACP, my son was born during the year – 2001 – researchers said marked the beginning of a trend that will see one third of black boys going to prison if nothing changes.

A first black (role model) president who is serious about prison and educational reform is an important step. Obama sounded serious about such things when I spoke with him before the South Carolina primary. His record in Chicago provides evidence that he is. But it won't be enough to stop my son from becoming another statistic.

That responsibility remains mine.

Obama's Support Not About Race

A WOMAN CALLED ME BEFORE the January S.C. Democratic primary. She would not be voting for Sen. Barack Obama because Oprah Winfrey "made it about race" by endorsing him. Never mind that Winfrey had never before endorsed any candidate, black or white.

"I was giving Obama a serious consideration in the beginning. Now I see 80 [percent plus] of black voters are voting for him and... I have to ask why," Jebadiah Locklear wrote on my blog. "It makes me think many or most of them are voting for him because he's black and no other reason. ... That stinks of racism to me."

Oh, the irony. Obama lost a race in his Chicago district in 2000 because he lost the "black vote" as his opponent – a black guy endorsed by Bill Clinton – painted him as being too cozy with white people. Now that Obama has become the first black Democratic presidential candidate to attract about 90 percent of black voters, in some primaries – some voters are concerned that makes him too black.

Let me say again: Obama is the first black Democratic candidate to attract this level of black votes and a significant number of white votes. White candidates have done it routinely.

Shirley Chisholm, who in 1972 became the first woman and first black person to run for the nomination of a major party ticket, couldn't. Neither could Al Sharpton, Jesse Jackson, Alan Keyes or Carol Moseley Braun.

Jimmy Carter, Michael Dukakis, Al Gore, John Kerry and Bill Clinton each received between 88 percent to 92 percent of black votes.

Think back to 1984. Jackson received about 77 percent of black votes. Obama is doing much better. That same year, Ronald Reagan got 71 percent of white Southern votes in the general election – 80 percent in Alabama and Mississippi – and 65 percent of overall white votes.

At the start of this campaign, Sen. Hillary Clinton held a 40-point lead among black voters. She was up by 25 points overall. Those numbers have shifted dramatically, with Obama up by 5 points to 11 points, depending on the day.

That means millions of black and white voters have gravitated towards Obama since this campaign began. Yet only the shift by black voters is seen as suspicious.

Some see 92 percent of black votes going to a black candidate and suspect racism or race-obsessed voters. America's majority-white population has chosen a white president 100 percent of the time.

Does that mean they are racist or race-obsessed?

Or have more nuanced and complex reasons and circumstances also guided them?

Affirmative Action Role Flickering

SENS. BARACK OBAMA and Hillary Clinton are making history. They are on the verge of ending affirmative action as we know it.

In 2003, then Supreme Court Justice Sandra Day O'Connor saved the policy for public institutions of higher learning while saying it had about a 25-year shelf-life. The success of Obama and Clinton has sped up the clock.

There's no denying racism and sexism remain, as do glass ceilings and unfair practices that slow progress.

There's no denying that studies have shown that quality is not affected by affirmative action and the policy does not promote widespread reverse discrimination. And there's no denying that women are still too often pigeonholed and minorities stereotyped and forced to navigate unique obstacles.

But Obama and Clinton proved – on the biggest stage in the toughest venue – that people determined to topple them can overcome obstacles.

It's one thing to dismiss the ascension of the first two black secretaries of state as a politically calculated move when President George W. Bush chose Colin Powell then Condoleezza Rice to fill that post. Too many have unfortunately done just that.

But it's harder to dismiss the general public. Obama and Clinton each received more than 7 million votes from a cross-section of America on Super Tuesday, and that after each garnered a couple million more in earlier contests. They both ended up with about 18 million each.

While the media has too often painted an overly simplistic picture of their campaigns as a referendum on race and gender, Obama and Clinton have received support from a diverse pool of voters. If that many Americans are willing to vote for them to become leader of the free world, how can we continue to believe racism and sexism can only be defeated with affirmative action?

Besides that, the open secret is that people like Obama and Clinton are the kind most likely to benefit from affirmative action even though they are the least needy – well connected, well-off and well-educated blacks and women. The truly disadvantaged are often left out because they've been forced to attend ratty schools and don't have the education to take advantage of such programs.

It's taken about 90 years for a woman to seriously challenge for the White House since women were allowed to vote, and about a half century for a black man to get this close after the passage of civil and voting rights legislation that guaranteed voting privileges for blacks.

And it was their talent and perseverance that brought them this far.

And it is that talent and perseverance that is pushing us further and faster than many thought possible.

Candidates' Diversity Is Just Right

VIRTUALLY ALL THOSE who have voted for him share his race. His coalition of supporters is the least racially diverse of the candidates still in contention.

By 2050 we are projected to be a majority-less nation, meaning the importance of being able to unite a collection of disparate voices and people is becoming increasingly paramount.

And if he were born into a different race, he would not be one of the finalists to become our next president.

That candidate is Sen. John McCain, not Sen. Barack Obama.

A black McCain, born in 1936, would not be potentially a few months from taking the oath of office to step into the White House.

He could not become president, no matter how well he braved Vietnam, no matter how much honor he would have shown during seven decades of life, no matter the amount of foreign policy experience, no matter how hardworking, qualified or capable.

He would not have risen to become a U.S. senator to earn the maverick moniker. He would even have had a hard time reaching the House of Representatives without a specially gerrymandered district.

Geraldine Ferraro, who blazed a trail in 1984 as the first woman on a major party ticket, said Obama was very lucky to be who he is.

"If Obama was a white man, he would not be in this position," she said.

She also said she would not have been a vice presidential candidate if she weren't a woman – though she didn't note that she would not have been given that opportunity 24 years ago if she were a black woman.

This kind of identity politics can be used to diminish anyone's accomplishments.

Sen. Hillary Clinton would not have been considered the front-runner before the first vote was cast if she weren't a white woman – because she would not be married to a former president, all of whom are white, which helped her become a U.S. senator. And a white rather than dark-skinned Obama would be comparable to former Sen. John Edwards, given that they both are intelligent, weren't born into luxury, are eloquent and don't have an expansive resume inside the Beltway (a trait that is overrated, anyway).

A white Obama wouldn't be making history or generating this much excitement. McCain, Obama and Clinton are powerful senators and the final three of a 303 million population who have a shot at becoming president.

Let's save the faux tears and pronouncements about how they face unfair challenges.

Life hasn't been too unkind to any of them.

Watermelon Slight Can't Spoil Historic Night

THE BLACK MAN WAS LYING on his back next to a Dumpster. Near his right hand was an empty KFC bucket, to his left pieces of watermelon. The picture was attached to a message titled: "Barack Obama's victory party."

It was part of a mass e-mail sent by a regular reader, maybe by accident, a reader who has told me a thousand times how much of a Christian he is, how racism is overblown, how it would go away if we just let it go. That was Monday. It's still in my inbox. I've wondered how to respond, or even if I should.

But on Thursday it didn't matter because even though that reader was using racist stereotypes to make fun of "Barack Obama's victory party," America's victory party was taking place in Denver.

Because as much as that e-mail – and the e-mail that said I wouldn't have this job if I weren't black – sting, they can't hold a candle to what took place last night, because it reminded me why America made it to this place. Because a countless number of people – white Americans and black Americans and Jewish Americans and Latino Americans and Native Americans – stood in the breach against racism, even when it wasn't convenient or comfortable.

Because they forced this country to live up to its ideals and wouldn't take no for an answer, even when it cost them their livelihoods, sometimes their lives.

Thursday night was America's victory party because

Obama was standing on the shoulders of Martin Luther King Jr. when Obama became the first black man to head a major party presidential ticket.

It was America's party because King stood on the shoulders of a white mother of six, Daisy Gabrielle, who stood in the breach. During the height of the civil rights movement, she took the hand of her elementary-age daughter, entered the "gauntlet of hecklers and shovers" – repeating the Twenty-third Psalm along the way – and walked into a school that had allowed in "a single Negro child," according to "The Race Beat," a book about the press and the Civil Rights Movement.

A woman told Gabrielle she was making a spectacle and sacrificing her neighbors.

"I told her when it comes to sacrificing my neighbors or my principles, I'd sacrifice my neighbors," she said. "Neighbors change; principles never do."

Thursday was America's victory party because Gabrielle stood on the shoulders of W.E.B. Du Bois, Ida Wells-Barnett and Archibald Grimke, black men and women; Henry Moskowitz, a Jewish man; Mary White Ovington, a white woman; Oswald Garrison Villard, a German-born white man; and William English Walling – a white man whose family once owned slaves.

They founded the National Association for the Advancement of Colored People in 1909 after an eruption of lynchings in Springfield, Ill., the place where Obama would, just short of a century later, announce his presidential campaign.

They stood on the shoulders of Jim Hoffman, a white Alabama farmer. In the early years of the 20th century, Hoffman stood in the breach. While many of his contemporaries participated in a de facto slavery - using the judicial system to re-enslave blacks up through the mid-1940s – or stood silently by, Hoffman testified about what he knew,

legitimizing the word of blacks who had told a grand jury of the rapes and beatings and murders they and others endured, according to "Slavery by Another Name."
Obama and King and all the rest stood on the shoulders of Sen. Charles Sumner of Massachusetts.

He's been described as the least racist man of his time, a time in which most others were either ignoring or excusing slavery. He was white. He pushed for the end of that peculiar institution. Pushed hard. He was one of the people, along with Frederick Douglass, who steeled the resolve of Abraham Lincoln.

They all stood on the shoulders of Crispus Attucks, a biracial man (black and American Indian) like Obama (black and white), who was one of the first martyrs of the American Revolution.

There are so many others, such as those who housed runaway slaves to help Harriett Tubman usher them to freedom. There are too many to name, too many who made a difference without making a headline. No matter how ugly things got, there were always Americans who stood in the breach, who reminded the country to hold these truths to be self-evident, that all men are equal.

Their shoulders were strong enough to provide the foundation upon which the 75,000 who showed up Thursday night stood to watch the first black man accept a major party nomination.

It's because of them that last night wasn't a political celebration – but an American one.

Blacks and Whites,
Brothers and Sisters

Holding To Divided Past Leads To Diminished Future

THE LITTLE BOY in the blue sweater held his right hand over his heart long after the soloist had belted out the final chord of the National Anthem.

He stood gazing as dignitaries and poets walked to the small glass podium to praise the African-American monument being dedicated outside.

The boy could be no more than 8 years old, but was head and shoulders taller than the young girl who stood by his side.

An American flag hung to their right, flanked by the 54th Massachusetts Volunteer Infantry Regiment, a re-enactment group serving as color guard.

They were surrounded by hundreds of mostly dark faces in the halls of a Statehouse that slaves helped build. Other children and adults lined the stairwells leading to the House and Senate chambers.

There large paintings depicting war and honoring S.C. heroes lined the walls. All but one of those pictured was white; a bust of Confederate icon Robert E. Lee and a statue of John C. Calhoun could be found at the top of the stairs.

The little boy was downstairs, staring into space, hand still over his heart, as the Hallelujah Singers sang, "What A Mighty God We Serve." His friend nudged him as Gov. Jim Hodges began to speak.

Hodges quoted Nelson Mandela, mentioned the names of S.C. greats and lesser-knowns, and said the

Statehouse was the first black monument because of the slaves' work.

Sen. Darrell Jackson, D-Richland, took his turn at the podium, saying the monument represents what is good about humanity and this state.

The little boy said nothing as his eyes darted out over the crowd.

"Until a future generation achieves more than we achieve, we cannot be a success," Jackson said, challenging all in the crowd to "place a child on your shoulders" to inspire them to new heights.

By then, the little boy had found a seat on the floor behind the podium. From there he heard Nikky Finney, author and daughter of the first black Chief Justice in South Carolina, read a poem.The monument represents but 12 chapters of a million-chapter book, the poem said.

Outside in the sometimes pouring, sometimes drizzle of a rain, other statues and markers commemorated a different view of S.C. history: the statue of U.S. Sen. Strom Thurmond; the marker recognizing the Robert E. Lee highway; Confederate Gen. Wade Hampton on his horse; the statue that honors the S.C. Women of the Confederacy; the marker commemorating the former Statehouse, which was burned during the Civil War; the monument in memory of the soldiers who fought in the Mexican War and the Spanish-American War; the statues of George Washington, Benjamin Tillman; and J. Marion Sims, founder of gynecology who was said to have been a doctor to both slave and empress.

On another section of the Statehouse grounds, the African-American monument stood covered in dark plastic. The coverings would later be removed to reveal stones from four places in Africa -- the Congo, Ghana, Sierra Leone, and Senegal --from where slaves were shipped to Charleston.

It charts a 400-year history through a series of connected sculptures showing a slave auction block, a slave ship and slaves working in a field.

The sculptures depict proud, dark-skinned fighters in a war, and scenes of Jim Crow and the 14th and 15th Amendments, and Brown v. Board of Education, and sharecropping and men and women carrying briefcases and playing horns — and one of an astronaut.

A woman among the hundreds touching and taking pictures of the monument said the raindrops bouncing off the sculptures made it seem as though our ancestors were crying.

Back inside, as Finney spoke about how there were once chains around our necks, how we were handcuffed in pairs, and how our dead were thrown overboard or buried in mass graves at Sullivan's Island, the little boy cracked his fingers.

Finney went on to the applause of an enthusiastic crowd to say we were never slaves, that we were only enslaved, and that black midwives pulled us into this world when others didn't want to touch us.

The little boy rubbed his eyes, seemingly oblivious to Finney's words about granddaddies hanging from trees like kudzu, or the fight of Joe Frazier and the flight of astronaut Ronald McNair.

After a benediction and applause, and as people filed out to view the monument, the little boy sat for a while, threw his head back and fixed his eyes above.

Maybe he was giving thanks, maybe pondering what he'd heard? I don't know.

As I watched him, I was praying for a day when debates over flags and paying homage to monuments would no longer get in the way of our need for each other.

I was praying for a day when our collective future becomes more important than our divided past.

White Southerner Spreads Powerful Black History Month Lesson

IT'S TWO DAYS before the end of Black History Month, and the thing I will remember most about these 29 days is my unexpectedly enlightening trip to the home of Robert Shelley of Shelley Construction.

His home has white columns, like those made famous by Southern plantations, and a Civil War cannon on his front lawn.

His doorbell rings "Dixie" and his dog is Scarlett, named after the character in "Gone With The Wind."

Inside, he has an old poster of "Amos `n' Andy." The show began in the 1920s and became the country's longest-running radio broadcast. Two white actors used their talents to voice dozens of stereotypical-sounding black and other characters.

It made its way to TV but was pulled in part because The National Association for the Advancement of Colored People and others said it relied too heavily on black stereotypes, though an influential black newspaper at the time, the Pittsburgh Courier, called the protests misguided and the show simply good comedy. According to the Museum of Broadcast Communications, white advertisers pulled out so as not to offend white Southerners by supporting the first TV show with an all-black cast.

Such is the messiness that is race. I touched on that messiness Sunday in reaction to a Black History Month program that included a speech by a pastor telling students to be proud of their blackness. The response was also messy.

I believe that the speaker did nothing wrong, just as I believe black history messages can be useful if done well, that Rush Limbaugh should not have resigned from ESPN, Don Imus should not have been fired and white students who want to display pride rather than hatred should be allowed to wear Confederate flag T-shirts to school.

We dumb down the American conversation with attempts to remove every potential offense from the public square. That's why I enjoyed Shelley's home, which was unabashedly full of Southern pride, of the Shelley kind. He has also spent several thousand dollars helping dark-skin people around the world through the humanitarian nonprofit Project Amazonas, which provides healthcare to the needy in places such as Peru. And he put an Egyptian girl through college.

Now he's trying to find the proper place for a slave gravestone. It was discarded during development of a former Georgetown plantation.

Shelley has the stone in his backyard. He said that though she didn't receive respect during life, she should be respected today.

"I want people to know that she lived," Shelley said.

Her gravestone will likely be placed at the restored Myrtle Beach Colored School, though Shelley still hopes a historian can help him track Saxby's lineage.

Her name was Rosetta Saxby. She lived from July 15, 1851 to Aug. 14, 1920.

A white guy who is "as Southern as it gets" is preserving her memory.

Black History Month messages such as that don't get much more powerful – or important.

Real History Isn't Sweet and Simple

MARTIN LUTHER KING JR. was killed 40 years ago today.

I graduated from Davidson College 13 years ago next month.

If not for the former, the latter wouldn't have been possible.

If not for the former, baby-faced Stephen Curry would not have carried Davidson to within 16 seconds of the Final Four, would not have energized a nation, most of which didn't know the small college was founded just north of Charlotte two and a half decades before the beginning of the Civil War.

Davidson began integrating in 1961, first with African students, then African-Americans. (Africans were expected to have an easier transition because they didn't have the racial scars of blacks who grew up in the South.) That was seven years before an assassin would find his mark on the balcony of the Lorraine Hotel in Memphis, but in the midst of a movement led by King that would change the world.

That movement, like King and integration in Davidson and elsewhere, didn't flourish because it was perfect. It flourished because it didn't blink when confronted with complexity and racial incongruity; it flourished because it had truth, in all its messy glory, as a foundation.

It wasn't perfect, just unflinching in the face of

challenge and discomfort.

The month King was killed, Davidson faculty, students and residents boycotted a local barbershop that refused to integrate. The barber was black and barred black customers for fear of losing his livelihood by offending white customers.

He was forced to make a dastardly choice. When I sat in a Davidson barbershop in the early 1990s, I didn't have to choose because people like King had already done the heavy lifting for me.

I sat among white and black men, white students and black students and international students. We all received haircuts from skilled black hands wielding scissors and shears.

We told off-color jokes.

We laughed together.

I imagine Curry is enjoying similar experiences. But so did long-forgotten Damon Williams, who lived on the other side of the tracks in Davidson, the side away from the prestigious private school, Main Street shops and nice homes.

Damon was a Love of Learning student, a summer enrichment program founded at Davidson by the Rev. Brenda Tapia to increase black college enrollment.

He was smart, outgoing and headed to college, just like most students from that program. But mentoring by black and white students and the concern from the college couldn't save him.

A couple of years after I graduated, he, like King, was killed by a bullet. It was from the barrel of a gun held by a police officer. A bullet from a gun Damon carried killed the officer. They died almost simultaneously.

His body lay in a ditch while the officer was attended to.

The Charlotte Observer carried the story and was

praised for the coverage of the officer's life – just as they undoubtedly were praised for the coverage of Curry and the basketball team's run to the Elite Eight – and criticized for documenting Damon's. He was a cop killer.

That's all readers wanted to know.

They didn't want to know what led him to that night or how the school tried to help him and so many others. They didn't want to know he was carrying a gun because he was afraid of the violence that had begun to engulf his world, in his neighborhood.

They wanted the story nice and neat for the same reason we universally praise King and quote his ``I Have A Dream'' speech on days like today while forgetting that during his life, he was often despised, considered too radical.

But to deny that complexity is to bastardize his story. It would be just as bad to forget Damon while celebrating Curry.

They Are My People Too

I EXPECTED we'd be the only three black people to
show up. It was a Friday morning, and I had taken my kids
to pick up tickets for the next night's Monster Truck event at
Myrtle Beach Speedway.

I had long spoken of taking them to a NASCAR race,
just hadn't gotten around to it, and I thought the Monster
Trucks would be the next best thing. The crowds would
be larger and more excited than the typical Saturday night
Speedway gathering, I figured.

We walked into the main office at the Speedway,
which resembled the kind of small wooden structures I'd
spent countless hours, while growing up, building with my
stepfather and brothers in our yard. Some were eventually
turned into bedrooms for tenants and mentally challenged
uncles. Some were used as storage. One was equipped with a
long hook to hang up the occasional disembodied hog to let
the blood drain before commencing with a barbecue.

There were at least three signs in the office reminding
us that cash transactions were the only kind accepted. A
large white man sat at a small brown table near a black-
handle phone on top of the kind of wood desk I sat in during
my elementary school years.

And there were white people in the line along with
us, as I expected. One man had dirty hands and a dirtier
T-shirt, as though he'd just pulled an engine from a car,
rebuilt it and put it back again. One blond woman looked like

someone's grandmother who had smoked three too many cigarettes in her life but displayed a smile that would make Miss Universe envious. Another woman spent four times as much on tickets as I did. She had a doting son in tow. After his mother purchased the tickets, he looked as though he had won the lottery.

In the meantime, the large white man at the small brown table was busy making small talk with my kids.

"How ya doin' big fella?"

"Fine," an unusually reserved Kyle returned.

"I know you are doin' fine, big as that smile is," he said, turning to Lyric.

"Yes," she said softly while nodding and smiling.

"You look familiar," he said, turning to me. "Where do you work?"

"The Sun News."

"I used to do some deliveries over there. That's where I know you from. I thought you looked familiar."

He flashed a welcoming smile before making small talk with others in the line. I made it to the counter.

"That'll be $55," the white ticket taker said.

I handed him the money.

"Are you that guy who writes the newspaper column?" he asked.

"Yes, sir."

"I 'm sorry, but I can't recall your name."

"Issac Bailey."

"Yeah, that's it. Just wanted to know I appreciate what you do."

"Thank you," I said before turning to leave.

"Some of those pieces, like the one on your cousin, or your brother, really get to the heart of things. They make people think. Like a friend of mine said, When you give a man the death penalty, you aren't hurting him, you're hurting his family."

He was talking about the series of stories and columns I did on how a murder my oldest brother committed 26 years ago changed my family, as well as the family of the man he killed. It surprised me, though it no longer should.

It surprised me because the stories had been published more than a year earlier – and because the ticket taker was white.

When I began writing such personal stories, I expected to hear from black families facing similar circumstances. And I did. But I also heard from many white families, some rich, some not so rich, some poor. They told me about loved ones who had committed rape or killed someone while driving drunk or who had shot someone in a fit of rage or who had committed crimes while members of the Ku Klux Klan … and how they had long carried the burden, silently, in shame, like my family did for 25 years before we finally sat down and faced the ugly.

The encounter with the Monster Truck ticket seller reminded me once again how easy it is for anyone to fall into traps of simplistic thoughts about race, about how even a lifetime of experience isn't enough to ward off such ignorance. I've studied race, been trained to conduct race relations seminars – even designed one myself – and still, those thoughts won't leave me without the occasional deliberate shove.

I expected to see only white people in the office because I had forgotten that race is a fallacy, that culture is the true reality. I liked Monster Trucks – the Ford Explorer Sport Trac, not a red Corvette, is my favorite vehicle – because I grew up in a rural part of South Carolina. We loved the legendary "Big Foot," long the king of Monster Trucks, and loved watching Wahoo McDaniel and Ric "Nature Boy" Flair and the "Junk Yard Dog" pummel each other in all-too-entertaining wrestling matches. I have fond memories of Bo and Luke and Daisy Duke, and Uncle

Jesse and Boss Hog, too. And I loved Minnie Pearl and her lampshade hat and that old banjo on "Hee Haw."

Being around white men in greased-stained T-shirts, or white women who had smoked too many cigarettes but smiled – without a dentist's recommendation – was nothing new, because on many days, while growing up, I wore greased-stained T-shirts to the grocery or convenience store to get a bite to eat during lunch break at Scotchman's, which served the best fried chicken this side of Pluto. My hands have been just as dirty, the underneath of my   Bunch family, the white man my brother killed, in a Georgia Pacific paper mill in Russellville, South Carolina. Fried chicken and fried fish and collard greens with ham hocks and barbecue and watermelon were staples for us all.

None of us was rich – well, except the white man who owned the IGA grocery store, the other white man who owned the furniture and hardware stores, and the black man who owned a nightclub (he found Jesus and converted it to a church) and an FM radio station, which was founded on Hip Hop and R&B but now plays gospel.

Those people I was in line with in the main office at the Myrtle Beach Speedway, and would be with the following night eating boiled peanuts and breathing in the fumes from Monster Trucks, were my people, as much as Barack Obama or Denzel Washington, or all the white and black people I grew up with in St. Stephen. Obama and Washington are my people, too, but they don't share my history, relish it, the way many of my white Southern brothers and sisters do.

The skin tone of the people in that office was different, yes, and in the South, maybe more than elsewhere, that means something, though not always what we expect. And that has sometimes led to misunderstandings and silly fights and unbridged divisions, but make no mistake, everything they are, so am I.

I'm unashamed that my vocabulary includes "ain't"

and "ya'll" and I say "South Carelina" instead of South Carolina, and sentences which say "That watermelon has fever in it" when it isn't just right or too ripe, and sentences that end in prepositions or are barely sentences at all, or that it also gives me the ability to debate the modern-day importance of Shakespeare and Chaucer or discuss why I'm captivated by the mapping of the human genome. (Please. Someone tell Hollywood producers that not everyone here speaks with a deep, Southern twang. Many of us don't, and some of us do, but only part of the time.)

I'm unashamed that I go to church alongside men who love the Confederate flag because while some of those men will swear, all evidence to the contrary, that slavery had nothing to do with the Civil War, they would happily give me the shirt off their backs or help my wife fix a flat in the pouring rain on the side of a busy U.S. 501 or watch my momentarily lost daughter with eagle eyes to make sure she's safe until she finds her way back to her mother on the beach.

And yes, sometimes-ugly stereotypes about black people slip out of the dark recesses of their brain, through their lips and into my ears. And sometimes they don't notice that they had, and other times don't care. And sometimes they love and support the Jesse Helmses and Strom Thurmonds a little too much and too long, and can be too wistful about the good ole days without remembering – or caring – that those good ole days weren't all that good for all of us.

But they are my people, too. Because they've laughed with me and cried with me and praised God with me and cursed me – and had me curse them right back – and been poor with me and struggled through under funded schools in the same way I have and been ridiculed for being born and raised in the South and underestimated because we don't walk or talk as fast as New Yorkers heading to the subway or a TV anchor behind a microphone. Because they've lived in mobile and manufactured homes and "slopped the hog" and picked tobacco just as I have.

And they've seen their boys go off to war in numbers similar to ours because military service has long been seen in our area as a way to make a good life, maybe even your best life, even more so than college or any other career.

And they've seen their boys go to prison alongside ours. Not in the same raw numbers or percentages, no doubt, but in numbers large enough that many of them have had to pack fried chicken, sweet tea and mashed potatoes into their wood-panel station wagons to have lunch on the prison lawn during visiting hours just like we have.

And they've seen the stable manufacturing jobs leave, making those who had parlayed a high school education into multimillion dollar companies fewer and farther between.

And they've felt the pain of a rusted nail through the bottom of their feet, or a heavy, rapidly moving hammer to the thumb, just as I have.

I'm not sure how things will change as the intersection of race and culture changes again, as has already begun to occur, with more brown faces showing up in our communities and workplaces, areas which had long been only black and white. But I imagine that they'll become my people, too, the growing Latino population that too many of my Southern brothers and sisters have reduced to ``those Mexicans.'' We'll laugh together, too, pray together, console each other … and fuss and fight with each other as well. Maybe soccer will substitute for some of the football games, but probably only a few.

In the main office at the Myrtle Beach Speedway, I temporarily felt out of place and expected to see only white faces because I had forgotten such things, forgotten that shared experiences are just as important – even more important – than a shared DNA or melanin level.

The ticket taker pulled me back to reality when he told

me how much he appreciated what I wrote. Those kinds of encounters always inoculate me against the rage and epithet-filled anonymous letters that find their way to me. They make it harder to lump white people together or to exaggerate the power racism has over my life.

We shook hands. I said thank you. As I walked out, the guy in the grease-stained T-shirt returned. He had slipped out to visit the ATM down the road. It was cash only and he only had credit cards.

We smiled at each other.

"I'm ready to go now," he said excitedly.

Outside, Lyric and Kyle noticed the white race car on display near the entrance to the Speedway. I turned back, just briefly, and noticed a couple heading into the main office, to get their tickets to enjoy the Monster Trucks.

They were black.

Proud, Not Blind

MY FATHER COULD have been a slave. That's
not a theoretical assertion. That's a fact. He was born 51
years after the official end of slavery but about three decades
before the end of a de facto slavery that enslaved maybe
200,000 black men in the American South during the same
period Hitler was killing and enslaving millions of Jews,
Gypsies, gays and other undesirables. Their physical bondage
was one of the tools used by racist, white Southerners to keep
millions of other blacks in a perpetual state of servitude.

Most of us know about the Jewish Holocaust, so
much so that the name Hitler is synonymous with the word
evil, that a symbol which had represented peace for centuries
before Hitler commandeered it – the swastika – is now
viewed in this country primarily as a reminder of some of
Earth's darkest days.

But almost none of us know about the South into
which my father was born, in 1916. I only know he was born
that year because of a document I found through ancestry.
com. My mother, who had been given away at the age of 13
to him by a father who could no longer afford to feed her and
her brothers and sisters, couldn't tell me. She couldn't hand
me his birth certificate because in the South into which my
father was born, black life was still viewed as unimportant,
except for the hard, ugly labor that could be hoisted upon
black backs for the betterment of that South, an ugly South, a
horrible South, particularly for a black man.

I was born in 1972 yet am only a generation removed from the days blacks (mostly men) were sold like chattel to companies who would literally work them to death, then replace them with others who were unfortunate enough to meet the same fate.

The South into which my father was born was a South in which the judicial system was designed to round up black men – more when private companies needed additional workers, less during economic downturns – charge them with bogus crimes, imprison them and sell them off to companies such as U.S. Steel and the Georgia Pacific Railroad Co. (My mother and stepfather worked for the Georgia Pacific wood plant in Russellville, S.C., as did one of my brothers, as well as a few members of the James Bunch family, the white man my oldest brother murdered.)

"Slavery by Another Name" lasted until World War II, Douglas A. Blackmon writes in a book by that title. They were charged with "changing employers without permission, vagrancy, riding freight cars without a ticket, engaging in sexual activity – or loud talk – with white women."

"By 1900, the South's judicial system had been wholly reconfigured to make one of its primary purposes the coercion of African Americans to comply with the social customs and labor demands of whites," Blackmon writes. "Revenues from the neo-slavery poured the equivalent of tens of millions of dollars into the treasuries of Alabama, Mississippi, Louisiana, Georgia, Florida, Texas, North Carolina, and South Carolina – where more than 75 percent of the black population in the United States then lived."

There were the gas chambers in Germany for the Jews. There were also numerous camps, which consisted of able-bodied Jews used as slaves. In the South into which my father was born, there was false imprisonment based on laws drawn up in former Confederate states, designed specifically to target black men. There were chain gangs of these men –

some laws were careful to specify that white prisoners not be humiliated by having to be chained to black men – and there was death. By the fourth year of the "prisoner leasing program" in Alabama, for instance, 45 percent of those men had been killed. "Company guards were empowered to chain prisoners, shoot those attempting to flee, torture any who wouldn't submit, and whip the disobedient – naked or clothed – almost without limit," Blackmon writes. "Over eight decades, almost never were there penalties to any acquirer of these slaves for their mistreatment or deaths."

"Whites realized that the combination of trumped-up legal charges and forced labor as punishment created both a desirable business proposition and an incredibly effective tool for intimidating rank-and-file emancipated African Americans and doing away with their most effective leaders."

They were stolen, this time not off the coast of Africa with the help of opposing African tribes, but off the streets in my native state of South Carolina and elsewhere throughout the South with the help of Ku Klux Klaners posing as judges and juries, constables and sheriffs. They were ostensibly given the death penalty – first, with hard, back-breaking labor – for having been born black, in America, into the South of which I'm now proud of but not blinded by. They were beholden to people who viewed them as subhuman, to people who murdered them and raped them and enslaved them in the same way – and at the same time – Jews were murdered and raped and enslaved in Germany. Only, Hitler thought Jews so unworthy he wanted them stricken from the face of the earth, while white racists in the American South thought blacks only worthy to do the bidding of whites, forced by consent of law and the presence of the horse whip to keep them in line.

Why do we know so much about the Jewish Holocaust – and rightly display inexhaustible compassion for those who survived it, as well as those who followed them – and so little about the Black Holocaust that was taking place on our own soil? Why do we appreciate the stories from Jewish survivors but scoff when black American victims recount their own stories?

My father – not my great-grandfather, not my ancestors from Africa, but my biological father – was born into a South in which the judicial system was literally and purposefully used to enslave black men, to tear apart black families, to keep them under a constant threat of terror and humiliation. It was full-blown terrorism on our soil decades before Sept. 11, 2001.

In that South, lynching was common. Blacks who had worked hard to become doctors and lawyers and elected officials were put back in their place through white mob violence, violence that included, or was approved by, a white-run government.

My father was born into that South. I don't know if that's why he beat my mother so often, or why it seemed, to him, an OK thing to do, or if it was why he drank so much. I don't know how living through that kind of nightmare changed men, don't know what it did to my mother, born much later, to live with a man trying to navigate that South, don't know what it did to other men like him, and other children like me.

This isn't ancient history. That South, that ugly, horrible South into which my father was born lives on in the hearts and minds of some of its survivors just as vividly as the Jewish Holocaust lives on in the hearts and minds of those who survived that hell a continent away. That South is not dead, and it never will be, no matter how many wish such unpleasantness could be wiped away with denial or a Southern pride devoid of reality.

I'm proud but not blind.

My father could have been one of the men stolen

and sold to a U.S. company. I should feel grateful that he wasn't, but can't help but wonder how his scars impacted me and my brothers, and if they were part of the reason our life outcomes – a convicted murderer, an air traffic controller, a writer, a truck builder, a car salesman, three others in and out of jail for dabbling in the drug and violence trade – were so disparate, so contradictory.

He grew up in a South which allowed a finite number of possibilities for black men like him while heaping an unknowable amount of burdens and hurdles, a South into which the word nigger was backed up by force of law and the noose. I'm raising my kids in a South in which one of my biggest challenges is dealing with people who think it somehow unpatriotic and divisive to mention that I'm black. The possibility of being lynched or sold into neo-slavery never crossed my mind. My South and my father's South aren't the same place but overlap nonetheless.

My father raised us in a South in which the possibilities slowly, but surely exponentially grew while most barriers disappeared – or were torn down by brave men and women. I was raised, and am raising, my kids in a new South, one in which the psychic scars are still prevalent, and both the progress accomplished, and the progress still needed are obvious.

"Is there something wrong with being black?" my six-year-old son Kyle asked.

We were about to feast on a roasted chicken and fried potato dinner at Medieval Times, a popular Myrtle Beach attraction consisting of knights, horses, kings and princesses. It was the 10th anniversary of the day my wife and I married.

The night of Kyle's question, we were using complimentary tickets given us by a family who has served as a de facto group of aunts and uncles for Kyle. That family is white and includes a former colleague. She was one of the first people we allowed to baby-sit our first-born.

We were in the cheering section for the Yellow Knight. Beside me was a white family. In front of us were other white families. Next to them were other white families. I caught a glimpse of a black man walking back to his table with what seemed to be his wife and child. Our server was a young black guy. One of the Knights' helpers on the jousting floor was another young black guy.

Besides that, the place was full, mostly of white people. Kyle noticed, as he has begun to notice more frequently since turning five.

"What?" I asked him, screaming a bit over the noise and the narrator.

"Is there something wrong with being black?"

"Why did you ask that?"

"Because there is only white people in here."

"Does that bother you?" I asked, knowing that he has spent most of his young life primarily in the company of white people when not at home.

He shook his head no, then yes.

"Why?"

"I don't know."

"Well, if you think of it, you can tell me."

He nodded his head, then took a sip of soda. That was the end of the conversation.

We enjoyed the rest of the show, cheered loudly for the Yellow Knight, watched as he vanquished two foes before being vanquished by a third. The prince was the final man standing. He was dressed in white. All white.

We walked out of the jousting area and through the souvenir section and past a small dance floor. The DJ – I believe she was a youngish-looking white woman – was blasting Snoop Dogg through the surround sound system.

"Snoop Doggy dooooog," I hummed to myself as we left among the throng of white people Kyle noticed.

Kyle's question got me thinking. What does it mean

for a little black boy to grow up in the South today, at least
this part of it?

I grew up in St. Stephen, S.C., then population about
900. I grew up in a large black family with two sisters, nine
brothers and an army of aunts, uncles and cousins, all black.
I attended a high school that was almost all black. One white
girl, a close friend of mine, graduated in my class, in 1991. I
graduated fourth. She was valedictorian, which displeased
one of our black teachers. That teacher had ``warned'' us
years earlier about that possibility, of having the only white
student finishing at the top of class.

It didn't displease us, her classmates. Jenee was a
friend. We knew she was smart. She kept us on our academic
toes just as much as we kept her on hers. And contrary to
reports from elsewhere – about academic excellence being
derided among black students as acting white – we were the
cool ones because our grades were so high, our prospects so
strong. Jenee and her white skin were admired for academic
achievements just as me, my black skin and my academic
success were admired, held in high esteem, in that almost all
black, rural South high school.

I think the teacher who warned us about Jenee was
afraid of what people would think for the same reason later
in life I avoided eating stereotypical black foods in front of
white people and was in near panic mode when I failed my
first psychology test at almost all white Davidson College in
a class in which I was the only black student.

But in my younger years, I was surrounded by black
people in the way Kyle, and my four-year-old daughter Lyric,
never have. My high school football team was mostly black,
with the occasional white student finding his way onto the
field. It was so black we were suspicious of two black guys
who played for Hananah High School, a small, public school
in the Charleston area. They were the only two blacks on an
almost all white team.

It was an unexpressed assertion that they somehow had sold out, even though we knew little about their background and ignored the obvious, that in South Carolina, attendance zones determined where you attended public school, not choice. It was funny how that suspicion was turned on its ear in college. I was one of a handful of black guys on an almost all white Davidson football team. I wondered what the football players at J.C. Smith, a historically black college in Charlotte, N.C., about 20 miles from Davidson, thought of me.

But in my younger years, there were black people in my midst. Black teachers, black people at the "light company," black people walking down the sidewalk, on the asphalt at the park, behind the counter and in the drive thru at Hardee's and at the mechanic's shop and in the pulpit and in the tobacco field and on the pictures on the wall. There were white teachers and cops, white businessmen and council members, for sure. St. Stephen wasn't all black, not nearly, but it was easy to stay in the majority.

For Kyle and Lyric, it's not that way. We live in one of the few areas in the country in which the white population is growing, by percentage and raw numbers, faster than the black population. It is becoming whiter even as the country fast approaches the day in which the population will be majority minority. Our church is mostly white, as is our neighborhood. The integration – predominantly white integration – is so prominent here and elsewhere in the South that courts will soon have to rethink what constitutes a properly gerrymandered Congressional district.

I tell myself that race isn't supposed to matter, that people are people, that good ones and bad ones come in all shapes, sizes and colors. I once convinced myself that color blindness was possible and ideal. I no longer believe it's possible, necessary or even desirable.

Kyle's questions kept forcing me to face the

contradiction that is race, for race surely is a contradiction. It exists even though it's not real. It has neither a definitive biological or sociological meaning. It means one thing to one group, something completely different to another, and even more perversely, different things to the same person, depending on the time in which they live or the mood they are in.

The Census Bureau, which for the longest time only had a few boxes to allow Americans to pick a racial category, had to relent in 2000 and allow 63 combinations. In Brazil, they stopped counting after the combinations numbered in the 200s. Barack Obama is black like me and white like Jeff Foxworthy.

Yes. That is a contradiction. But there is no other sane way to understand race. And that's why my parenting will be full of contradictions, as is my pride for the South.

Kyle and Lyric are growing up in a South I didn't know as a little boy. I picked tobacco and cucumbers for summer jobs. I had a dirt bike and Go-karts and muddy roads to enjoy them upon. I ate watermelons full of little black seeds, some of which we grew in our back yard. They have Medieval Times and Dolly Parton's Dixie Stampede, during which a fictional South fights against the North, a show we love, a show full of patriotism rivaling anything in Boston or Philadelphia. It's a celebration of the South, and America, in the context of a war that saw the South almost tear the country in two. And they hardly know what to do with a watermelon that isn't seedless.

Kyle and Lyric are attending schools in which they are in the racial minority. And if we don't move, that will likely be the case through high school. My school was poor, black, under funded. It no longer exists. It was replaced in an attempt to desegregate – four decades after Brown v. Board of Education.

My children's schools are mostly white and

sufficiently funded and well stocked. But not too far away, across the county line, too many black boys and black girls – and a growing number of poor white and Latino ones – are locked into schools where ceilings fall on their heads, where snakes and rodents crawl through holes in the wall after heavy rain storms, where the bulk of teachers are under prepared and under paid, no matter their level of dedication.

My kids go to the kind of school I could only have dreamed about while I was growing up. Other kids their age go to the kind of schools – in forgotten rural areas – I matriculated through, sometimes worse. They all live in the South. Both their conditions – not just one – define the region I love, of which I am proud but not blinded by.

Kyle and Lyric are living during a time in which the level of black education has never been higher, the amount of black graduates never greater, the black middle class never larger. They can bump into black doctors, lawyers, dentists and elected officials on the street and not have to bat an eye. It's that commonplace. They have white friends who hug them in public as though they were long, lost friends, and have tea parties in their homes. They have white neighbors who voluntarily offer to allow their father to use their weed eaters and edgers, just because. They have white people who know them through my column, love to see them smile, and white people who don't mind protecting them like guardian angels on the beach, making sure no harm comes their way if they find themselves momentarily lost.

The house in which they live is bigger than the one my eight brothers and two sisters and host of cousins lived in not so long ago. And my brother's house in Atlanta is even larger. Brown-faced men with foreign tongues have sweated while putting up sheetrock in our house and a privacy fence around my brother's in-ground backyard pool.

And those underfunded, rural schools provided us the education we needed to make those realities happen.

There were no Advanced Placement courses, no state-of-the-art equipment, and in large measure, not even an up-to-date library. But there were good teachers – a few of them great – and a dedication to arm us to succeed in an unfair world. The South in which we live is prosperity, too; it's equality, too; it's beautiful, everyday cross-racial exchanges, too.

But the overall graduation rate in South Carolina and other Southern states remains static and too low, sometimes even going in the wrong direction. The incarceration rate remains too high, and the rise out of poverty remains too steep a climb. And too many in the General Assembly are blinded by the Confederate flag, so much so that they stubbornly insist that it must remain on the State House grounds in Columbia even while it continues to harm our image and means we won't be allowed to have the kinds of lucrative bowl football games so many other states enjoy.

It's a South that can adequately prepare young black boys and young black girls to become president of the U.S. while making it almost impossible they can make it there from this perch. A U.S. Senate seat and the governor's office are the two main roads to the White House. In South Carolina, a black man or woman hasn't come close to gaining either position.

My father was born into a South in which the judicial system was designed to intimidate and terrorize people who look like him because he had dark skin and the South – and for the longest time this country – made being black a sin punishable by death and torture. I was born into a South in which half my brothers found themselves in jail or prison, primarily because of their actions. My kids are living in a South, in a state where the kind of justice system reform needed to minimize the incidents of wrongful convictions are slow in the coming because too many prosecutors and elected officials seem more enamored with high conviction rates than true justice.

My kids are living in a South that is gorgeous, with
white sand beaches and palmetto trees and great live oaks
dotting the roads. It is rich in history and tradition. It is a
place in which my kids can legitimately believe they can be
trained as astronauts or scientists even as researchers have
documented time and again that being black makes them
more suspect and more likely to get caught in the juvenile
justice system, not only because of their actions but because
of "negative race effects." That's a reality the South shares
with the rest of the country.

"Nationwide, in every offense category – person,
property, drug, public order – African American youth were
disproportionately detained," according to the "And Justice
For Some" juvenile justice system study.

It's not de facto or "slavery by another name" all
over again, but there are too many parallels. Black kids are
more likely than white youth to be formally charged even
when referred for the same type of offense. More than three-
quarters of drug cases involving black youth result in formal
processing compared to just over half of whites in similar
cases. White youth are more likely to be placed on probation
while black youth more likely to be sent to an institution.

"When white youth and African American youth
were charged with the same offenses, African American
youth with no prior admissions were six times more likely to
be incarcerated in public facilities than white youth with the
same background," researchers found.

Black youth make up 28 percent of juvenile arrests
– but 58 percent of those admitted to state adult prison.
That's true, not only for the South in which I'm raising my
children, but for the country as a whole. The South, it seems,
has caught up with the rest of America. Or maybe the rest of
America has caught up with the South.

"While 'Equal Justice Under the Law' is the
foundation of our legal system, and is carved on the front

of the U.S. Supreme Court, the juvenile justice system is anything but equal for all," the "And Justice for Some" researchers found. "Throughout the system, youth of color – especially African American youth – receive different and harsher treatment for similar offenses."

The South into which my father was born, a South in which he could have been enslaved, isn't that far removed from the South in which I'm raising my kids. But like race, the South remains a contradiction. The possibilities and opportunities are endless even as the hurdles and injustices remain numerous. That excites me and scares, makes me proud and apprehensive.

That's why I'm proud of the South but not blinded by it. My kids won't have to leave, won't have to escape to a better life in the North. They can live here the rest of their lives and accomplish whatever they put their minds to.

But I also know the South Carolina prison population is about two-thirds black –mostly un- or undereducated men – in a state in which the population is only one-third black, a state whose educational system still lags too far behind. I know that while the opportunities are endless in this new South, we still have a weak governor's office because racist white men long ago looked at the high concentration of blacks in South Carolina, feared the possibility of a black governor and stripped the office of much of its power, just in case. I know that it is rare for a black person to be elected to statewide office, or that only a couple of blacks have served on the S.C. Supreme Court.

I know that my kids still might encounter a teacher who takes a look at their dark skin and assumes they can't be brilliant. I know that they still might be called nigger.

And I know that, given all those contradictions, it's not hard to understand why it's reasonable for my children to wonder, aloud, if there is something wrong with being black in a South that has come so far from its ugly past but still has so far to go.

Family

Real Life
Can't Be Explained
By Racial Theory

TODAY'S COLUMN WILL be short and sweet.

If it went any longer, too much of the anger trying to ooze from my fingers will find its way into print. And all my focus would be lost along with it.

I'm angry that the world isn't perfect. That good people do bad things. That I can't, with the stroke of a pen, wipe evil from the earth.

That it's hard, sometimes seemingly impossible, to get people to realize this: We are 99.9 percent alike. Scientists told us that recently, but those paying attention knew that long ago.

But too many don't pay attention, don't understand that when they explain away someone's actions by noting their skin color or circumstance, it is akin to handing God back the $100 bill He's given them in exchange for a 10 cents piece, and being proud of the trade.

How silly is that?

Which brings me to the more complicated discussion of Black History Month.

Is it still necessary is a growing question. I won't answer that. Can't.

But I know it was founded as a week and grew into a month because so many in this country had become infatuated with 10-cent pieces.

Yet it has the potential to keep us caught in a time warp.

For the people whose accomplishments are being highlighted didn't achieve those things because of melanin-rich skin. Something more powerful guided them.

But is there a better way to acknowledge what's long been overlooked? You tell me. I'm not smart enough to figure it out.

Because I know a family. My family. The uninformed would say black family.

I say a family complete with a convicted murderer, an investment advisor, a member charged with possession of marijuana and crack cocaine, another an air traffic controller, another victimized by drive-by shootings, another a writer, another who drank himself to death, another a great father and husband, another the victim of domestic abuse, another who has built a successful life and several businesses with a third-grade education.

Explain that with current theories about race and circumstance.

I'm waiting.

The Nightmare Lives On

I WAS 9 YEARS OLD when my oldest brother became a murderer.

It was a dark night, I was told. There was a robbery, 48 stab wounds and an arson fire. Some 19 years later it all seems like a bad dream, a nightmare from which I'll never wake.

It all seemed more real the past weeks as I followed the proceedings of the capital murder case of James Nathaniel Bryant III, who savagely beat and shot to death Horry County police Cpl. Dennis Lyden.

Lyden's wife has been mourning him for several years now; Bryant is scheduled to die for his crimes. Me? I haven't been able to reconcile that night of almost two decades ago.

I can't get over trying to remember the man I knew Moochie was with the man who, high on speed, allowed evil to step into his heart and through the tip of a knife's blade.

I loved my brother because he talked to me, kept the bullies away, and bought me ice cream.

I never saw the rage inside him that could take a life. Many days, I don't know if I should feel love or hate.

Many days, I feared myself, thinking what was hiding deep in him could also be hiding in me.

It was my biggest deterrent from dabbling in drugs or alcohol. For too many years, I saw my mother blame herself, being tortured with questions of where she went wrong, of how she could have been a more perfect parent, about why she didn't see it coming. Never mind she raised 10 others to be kind and compassionate, to respect life, even if not every one of us heeded her guidance.

I heard similar questions from Bryant's father.

"This is not what me and my family are about," he said as he pleaded with the jury to spare his son's life. "If I could give my life so that Officer Lyden could come back I would."

I believe him.

For too many years I thought little of Mr. Bunch, the man Moochie confessed to killing. Never considered how his family had been ripped apart, how their faith in humanity would be forever shaken.

Seeing photos of Mrs. Lyden fall uncontrollably into the arms of friends as she listened to details of how her husband was violently taken away from her reminded me of that.

But I still don't quite know what it all means.

I can tell you my faith requires that I don't let circumstances, no matter how dastardly, be my guide.

I can tell you that as a journalist I've had to call friends and family of victims of violent crimes – knowing we must shed light on the good and evil in this world – yet despised having to do it.

I can tell you that as a 9-year-old boy, I didn't understand evil, and how it destroys and devastates so much more than what it touches.

I want to explain to you why people do what they do, why someone can allow evil into their soul.

I want to give you some great insight into why killers kill, write that I've learned something from what happened 26 years ago.

I want to tell you things to answer all your questions, assure you there's something we can do to make certain it doesn't happen again.

I can't. My understanding doesn't run that deep. But I do know this. Evil, in but an instant, changed the course of two families last year when Lyden pulled the car Bryant was driving.

Only love can put them back on track.

Family's Troubles Continue

I BELIEVE IN BEING OPEN and honest, even when it hurts or is embarrassing, so I won't stop now.

I got the least surprising, yet disturbing, phone call. Unsurprising because I've long feared receiving such a call, disturbing because I was praying it would never come.

My nephew, Albert Harris, and my brother, James McDaniel, were charged in the murder of a 29-year-old Jamestown man.

The cops flooded my mother's yard and house and interrogated her, demanding to know where my brother and nephew were. It was 25 years ago all over again, a quarter of a century since the day my oldest brother was sought for a murder for which he continues to serve time in prison.

My brother and nephew turned themselves in.

I'm hoping there is some kind of mistake, some kind of mix-up. I'm hoping that this isn't really happening again.

I want the victim's family to be consoled, comforted.

I want the presumption of innocence to remain paramount.

I want them to have a fair trial. I want to love them but am having a hard time figuring out how.

I, like my mother and other siblings, have tired of driving hundreds of miles every year to attend parole hearings for my oldest brother at a designated S.C. prison, knowing that they all end the same way, within five minutes and with a denial. And so far, I've only visited my brother and nephew once since their arrest, not knowing what to say or do.

I don't want to dwell on it, for fear that a sense of helplessness will set in, because I understand that contrary to the most-overly simplified notion on the planet – that all it takes are positive role models in young black men's lives to save them – that every "good" decision my oldest siblings made – staying out of trouble, finishing our education, starting careers and families – created barriers, not bonds, between us and our youngest, most troubled loved ones.

The irony is that the person who had the best shot of convincing them to steer clear of trouble was my oldest brother. Their mutual jail and prison experiences bonded them in ways that separated them from the rest of us. We grew up in the same house but somehow ended living and walking in different worlds.

But I also want to tell you that, as hard as it may be for you to believe, they are not monsters, they are not beyond redemption, even though they've made more poor choices than I can count. They are children of God who live by a code I don't pretend to understand.

Desire To Be White Just Momentary

IT WAS IN DECEMBER that my 6-year-old son Kyle stunned me.

He asked if the nigger was bad. He had heard it uttered by a giggly boy performing a freestyle rap.

It was several days ago when he told me he wanted to be white.

"Sometimes I wish I was white," he said nonchalantly.

"What?" I returned, trying to sound nonchalant.

"Sometimes I wish I was white," he said again.

It's always been a silent fear of mine, that my kids would get sucked into believing the abundant societal messages that suggest there is only one way to be beautiful.

Kyle's comment momentarily confirmed that fear. It was particularly unnerving because I recently had a conversation with a colleague. It's a myth, I told her, that young generations would automatically handle race better. She had alerted me to an article that showed that young folks also harbor racial stereotypes.

Older folks teach younger folks, and that includes how we respond to race, even when we aren't purposefully passing along our hang-ups.

I vowed to never assume that my kids would view the world as I did, or even that they should. I said I wouldn't force the issue but neither would I be too uncomfortable to answer their questions.

Kyle's comment provided another test. He told me

he counted the black and white students in his class. He said it was mostly black. (His school is mostly white.) He once described a blond boy as black because the boy was wearing a black T-shirt.

"Why do you want to be white?" I asked.

"Sometimes I still want to be white because there are more white people," he said. "And if I was Braxton, I would get more Capri Sun. He gets Capri Sun in his lunchbox every day. I wanted to get Capri Sun so bad, then I started thinking if I was white, I would get more Capri Sun."

"But I give you Capri Sun," I said.

"Yeah, but you just started doing that."

Brice, who is white, is his best friend. He also plays with DeAndre, Charlie, Marshall, Hannah, Nina and Daniel. Some are white, others black.

"And when I looked at Michael Jackson, I thought he was white," Kyle said. "I thought I would be a better dancer if I was white."

"But Michael Jackson is black," I said.

"I still think I have to be white to dance like him because you haven't proved that he's black yet."

He continued: "When I'm white, then I might want to turn back to brown."

"Why?" I asked.

"Because nobody would know that I'm Kyle."

I Want to Laugh With My Brother Again

GOT A LETTER FROM MY OLDEST BROTHER, the one who had been in prison for 19 years by that point after being convicted of first-degree-murder.

Only, he didn't write the letter. Someone I vaguely know did. He changed his name and soul some time ago.

When he left us and I was nine, he was Moochie.

Mtume writes today, and Moochie is nowhere to be found. And I believe the 9-year-old in me feels cheated.

Cheated by him, by the justice system, by evil – by all those fools who actually say prison is too easy.

They don't know about the large rats scurrying around Moochie's feet at night, the pepper spray bath he received, or the constant moving from barbed-wire hell to barbed-wire hell, not knowing when or if he'll see a smile from a family member again.

They don't know about the night we received a prank phone call telling us someone had killed him. But I'm not here to write about how ugly and unfair prison is. Criminals should pay for their crimes.

I'm here to tell you about a man I call my brother, though I don't know him. I remember the days we jogged together, talked about girls and music. How I laughed, my heart full of joy, because he was there.

I didn't know he was using drugs or getting into trouble hanging out with the wrong crowd. He was there, my big brother. That was enough.

His letter reminded me that man is long gone, for all it talked about was how I better not give my first child a slave name, how I needed to learn – and now! – more about Afro centricity, and the motherland Africa. About how I should get out of that integrated church. About how it was time for me to wake up, realize the truth about this world. All his thoughts and words flow from a place I've never visited, don't want to know.

But it's a place that's kept him sane, a place that has grown him into a man. When we first began to visit him long ago, he was angry. Hate became his comforter. Rastafarism, a religion foreign to my Christianity, has guided him through the bad days, of which there have been many.

During visits, I could see how his new faith had focused him on some bigger cause, focused his energy on uplift rather than the cold steel bars in front of him.

It lit a passion so deep it has become his only reason for living. The long, sun-drenched dreadlocks that have become the outward expression of his faith are the very things prolonging his stay in prison.

A mid-1990s S.C. law called for all prisoners to have closely cropped hair. Mtume refused a haircut, and Moochie has been in solitary confinement ever since.

I'm angry with the system about that, angry that prison officials are so blind they can't see that law is threatening the one thing that has made Moochie a better man, the one thing that will make him a better citizen.

Hard drugs and unfocused men and women aren't allowed in his faith.

But I feel ashamed of myself as well, for though I know about how he needs that hair and that strange faith, all I want is my brother back.

Want to sit down, if only for a minute, and laugh again with the one who was here before the handcuffs and chains took him away.

One Memory of Father Floods Back

I'VE LONG HATED MY FATHER.
For as far back as I can remember, I thought of only a few things when my mind wandered to him, the events inscribed on my brain like movie scenes on DVD.

I always remembered the time he beat my mother in the kitchen. In all the memories I'm scared, powerless and young, I just don't know how young.

I always remembered the time he relentlessly beat my brother and me for playing in the bed of his truck. He used his leather belt, or a drop cord. I always remembered the time he smashed my favorite toy, a yellow Tonka, on a cold Christmas morning.

"Shouldn't left it in the driveway," he said with a gruff voice as I cried.

I always remembered the Mallo Cups. After my parents divorced, my mother would force us to visit him. She said his mother died during childbirth, and that it likely scarred him in ways we would never understand.

He lived in a run-down shack on the other side of the tracks. He gave us handfuls of the candy every time we went. I think it was his way of saying he was sorry for all the things he had done, and didn't do. But I only remembered the candy as being too sweet, too creamy.

I can't tell you why, but for the first time in ages this past weekend, I remembered something else. I don't know if it had anything to do with Father's Day, a time I usually spend reflecting on my own fatherhood, about how clueless I remain, about how I hope my kids don't notice I don't know what I'm doing.

But I reflected on why I let my kids play on the back of the truck and never once considered using a drop cord to discipline them.

And I hug and kiss them in the ways my father never did. I wanted to be everything he wasn't, I wanted my kids to know I would protect them in the ways he didn't protect me.

Then I remembered a winter night. My siblings and I, seven or eight of us, were huddled together in a makeshift bedroom added to our tin can of a mobile home, the kind known to burn so quickly many victims have been left in its wake.

A wood fire was burning.

I was in my underwear.

The room lit up, bright as day, an orange light through the window. My father rushed in, one pants leg on, the other dangling as he tried to grab it.

He made it outside. I heard what sounded like rain hit the side of the house. He had grabbed the water hose to fight a fire that had begun while we slept.

A few minutes later emergency officials were in our yard. But my father had put it out.

He had already saved us.

Spirits of Old Deserved to Hear: Change Has Come

I NEEDED TO BE WITH THE SLAVES.

As the election returns were coming in, I drove 42 miles to be in their presence.

I got there, Wedgefield Plantation, parked a few dozen feet from an old slave cabin, shut off my truck's engine, turned off the radio and sat in the dark.
Several dozen Spanish Moss-draped live oaks surrounded me.

I closed my eyes, said a prayer and a quick thank you. I'm not sure they heard me, but I said it anyway.

I had to pass dozens of other plantations to get there, plantations turned into golf courses, a plantation as a state bank, plantations as moderately and not-so-moderately-priced developments.

I glided along U.S. 17 and zipped past the former plantation property that is now Brookgreen Gardens. I was headed to the city where the nation's first black first lady has deep roots. I couldn't get there without first zipping right by the place where the discarded gravestone of Rosetta Saxby was found.

She lived from July 15, 1851, to Aug. 14, 1920. She spent the first part of her life as a slave and the second in a world adjusting – and not always well – to a new reality. That world changed again Tuesday night. That's why I had to be with the slaves.

And when I arrived at Wedgefield – and parked between that rotting former slave cabin and a pool house – I just wanted to sit there, just wanted to envision what they – the slaves who once lived there and worked there and died there and held onto hope there - would think if they could feel what I was feeling, experience what this country was experiencing.

I breathed in the silence of falling leaves, allowed myself to be comforted by the darkness, engulfed by the chirping of small critters, and just sat there, and stared.

The slaves weren't there, but their spirits never left.

I had to be the first to tell them the good news, had to share what was happening, had to let them know that what they never imagined was occurring. I had to tell them that a black man was chosen to lead the country that once enslaved them, had to tell them that we haven't forgotten that they were chosen to build this country's wealth through back-breaking, uncompensated labor, but now a man who shares the skin tone that caused them so much pain was chosen to preserve its prosperity.

I had to let them know that while they were demonized for having even a drop of black blood, the mixture of black and white blood running through his veins helped propel him toward the White House, that 63 million pairs of black, brown and white hands at the ballot box officially delivered him.

I wanted them to know that though their unkempt hair was deemed unattractive, he and his wife and two daughters are taking happy, nappy hair to 1600 Pennsylvania Ave.

They needed to know that while they lived days during which they were beaten for trying to learn, he rode the wave of one of the country's finest educations to sit atop the world's most powerful perch.

They needed to know that we haven't forgotten they

built the White House, and that he gets to rearrange
the West Wing.

They needed to know that though the courageous but
imperfect Founding Fathers didn't live up to their promises,
they embedded in the Constitution the ideals that made his
ascent possible more than two centuries later.

They needed to know that though we won't forget –
can't forget – we won't be the same.

No more can we deny the opportunities presented us.

No more can we take for granted the legacy that
stretches from the western shores of Africa to a 47-year-old
born of a white Kansan mother and a black Kenyan father.

No more do we have the luxury of assuming the
worst because we are afraid that divided days of yesteryear
will mean divided days tomorrow.

No more can we remain slaves to a haunted past.

The Real Story Behind The Polls

I WON'T EVER FORGET the day I beat up Neil Floyd. It was during lunch at St. Stephen Middle School.

I was egged on by friends who said Neil "dissed" me. So I did what any clueless, immature boy giving into peer pressure would do. I jumped on him and punched his chest several times.

Neil seemed more annoyed than hurt. But what I didn't realize that day – and why too many in the media are missing a major story unfolding during the presidential campaign – is that I had breached an important wall in my friendship with Neil for something a lot less meaningful.

I had violated our trust, had unwittingly put our similarities and natural bond on hold in order to uphold a superficial racial expectation. Neil was white, one of the few white students who attended my school, the kind of student who knows little about the supposed "white privilege."

From early on, we connected. I can't tell you why. Maybe it was because he liked BB guns the way I liked BB guns, liked go-karts the way I liked go-karts, liked "The Dukes of Hazzard" the way I liked "The Dukes of Hazzard."

Maybe it was because I saw him wear worn jeans like I wore.

Maybe it was because I knew his family was no more well off than mine. Though he didn't play a lot at my house or me at his, I knew that his wasn't any more valuable than

144

the tin can of a mobile home I grew up in.

I knew I picked tobacco and cucumber, worked under the hood of cars in my driveway, walked around in grease-stained T-shirts after long days of work, jumped BMX and Huffy bikes off makeshift particle board ramps, and knew Neil did the same things.

We were the same in every way that mattered, except that race was elevated in ways it never should have been. Neil's parents eventually pulled him out of St. Stephen to attend Macedonia, which had more white students than black. Many white parents chose the same route, which is why my graduating class ended up being 99 percent black.

The same social mores that convinced them to ignore our similarities compelled me to pummel Neil that day in middle school. It felt more important to fall in line than to stand firm on a genuine cross-racial friendship.

But I know that if Neil and I crossed paths today and I needed help, he'd give me the grease-stained T-shirt off his back, as I would for him, even if a Confederate flag sticker resided on his truck bumper.

This nation remains imperfect even after decades of real progress. But working-class whites are showing that a focus on serious issues can trump superficial racial alliances.

Think back to the waning weeks of the Democratic primary between Hillary Clinton and Barack Obama. The common media narrative was that rural whites would have a hard time voting for Obama, in large part because of race.

That rationale intensified when Clinton won in states such as Ohio and Pennsylvania. The story line implicitly suggested that these white people wouldn't vote for a black man. They used polling data to back up the claim.

But look at the polls now. Obama is leading in Ohio and Pennsylvania primarily because many rural, white voters have flocked to support him.

And even in West Virginia – a state that was

relentlessly targeted with that stereotypical brush – the race has tightened in ways few predicted.

Dark-skinned Obama is only trailing McCain by seven percentage points among this demographic. White John Kerry and Al Gore lost by 23 points and 17 points, respectively, among this group.

The tide has changed so much that "Newsweek" penned this headline: "McCain losing ground with working-class whites."

It doesn't surprise me the way it might astound political pundits.

Because I remember Neil.

They never knew him.